Elusive Equality:

Liberalism, Affirmative Action, and Social Change in America

James C. Foster and Mary C. Segers
with
Mary C. Thornberry and Bette Novit Evans

National University Publications
ASSOCIATED FACULTY PRESS
Port Washington, New York

Manufactured in the United States of America

Published by
Associated Faculty Press, Inc.
Port Washington, New York

Library of Congress Cataloging in Publication Data

Main entry under title:

Elusive equality.

(Multidisciplinary studies in law and juris-prudence)
(National university publications)
  Bibliography: p.
  Includes index.
  1. Equality—United States—Addresses, essays,
lectures. 2. Affirmative action programs—United
States—Addresses, essays, lectures. I. Segers,
Mary C. II. Series.
JC575.E43   323.42′0973   81-18612
ISBN 0-8046-9309-9   AACR2

CONTENTS

PREFACE

We Americans started our career as an independent people with an ethos and a condition of equality that were a source of congratulation to ourselves, and a source of wonder to countless observers. Countless persons high and low, foreign and native born, have seen this as the land of both equality and liberty—the land which gave promise, as Lincoln put it, "that in due time the weights should be lifted from the shoulders of all men, and that *all* should have an equal chance."

That is only half the story, however. We Americans escaped the feudal rigidities and fixed inequalities of the Old World, but we have been marvelously fertile in replacing them with inequalities of our own invention—racial, sexual, ethnic, religious, occupational, and class-based disparities of income, wealth, and power that persist and harden over generations. Everywhere Tocqueville looked, except at slavery and the Indians, he saw equality, with more of the same still to come. The events, of course, have proved him nearly dead wrong about the future of equality in the United States, but approximately right about its future in Europe. While country after country in Europe have moved from a condition of narrow oligarchy and radical inequality toward ever more broadly based representative regimes and a large measure of social and economic equality, we, with minor exceptions, have moved in the opposite direction. Populism, the early New Deal, and the 1960s movements for more economic, racial, and sexual justice all tried to stem or reverse the antiequalitarian tide. All largely failed. Shortly before he died, Alexander Hamilton, who never concealed his elitist and anti-democratic sentiments, said that "this American world was not meant for me." Could Hamilton have lived on, he would surely now feel at home, while most of the other great founders—Jefferson, Madison, Paine, Franklin, even Washington—would just as surely find themselves strangers in a strange land.

We have of course preserved much of the old public creed of equality even while moving toward inequality. As the gap between creed and reality widens, we try to close or conceal it by rhetoric. During the last ten to fifteen years especially, the rhetoricians of the corporate and political worlds have been joined by a host of academics and publicists who are showing us that the whole question of moving toward equality is so fraught with practical, philosophical, and moral perplexities and dangers that it is best that we stop where we are. These writers, many of whom will be met in the present book, are adepts at whitewashing, and even celebrating, departures from the democratic path by sophisticated doublethink and doubletalk. I think we are meeting more of that kind of ideology today than at any time since the late nineteenth and early twentieth century Social Darwinists and eugenicists did their share in throwing the mantle of Lockean individual liberty over the capitalist corporation, and in showing that the poor and the outcasts were exactly where they deserved to be.

Nowhere is there more of this doubletalk and doublethink than in recent neoconservative arguments against genuine affirmative action and equality of opportunity. It is truly amazing how many writers have recently tried to convince us that we now have about as much equality of results and equality of opportunity—to employ the fashionable and factitious polemical opposites—as we ought to have, and that efforts to get more can only jeopardize almost everything else that matters, from liberty through civility and on to success in the struggle to survive in a hostile world.

And yet, of course, no amount of words can conceal the hard fact that opportunities are very far from equal, and that, despite all the impassioned arguments about affirmative action they are becoming less equal. Wealth still breeds wealth and poverty breeds poverty; the position of most blacks, despite the successes of a small upper middle class, has deteriorated over the past ten years; the conditions and life-chances of the poor, of women, and of many racial and ethnic minorities are threatened by rising unemployment and inflation. Despite the individual examples of meteoric social rise, which are part of the legend of our national epic, the inferior conditions and impaired opportunities of one generation are largely bequeathed to the next. And now the present national administration is announcing in every way it knows how that inequality of condition and opportunity is simply not among the concerns of the federal establishment. All those groups that met with considerable official sympathy in their struggle for social justice and fair treatment in the 1960s and early 1970s are now being kicked back into the closet. Whether they can be put and kept there is, I think, very doubtful; but there is no doubt at all that that is what most of our present masters intend to try.

The present book thus enters a long debate at an important moment. The author's own Introduction accurately describes the scope and intention of their work, and they do in the book what they say they will do in the Introduction. Furthermore, they are attractively modest in assessing their own success. I think their book succeeds admirably. The historical account of the development of ideas of equality and inequality in the United States, for example, is solid and thoughtful. The treatment of affirmative action programs is excellent. The chapter justifying equality is philosophically sophisticated and morally sensitive. They show throughout a keen awareness of the political, social, and ethical complexities of their subject.

These authors have written with the abilities of the scholar and the concerns of the citizen. Their command of the relevant empirical material is firm, their respect for careful argument is high. They know that the scholar on this subject, too, would not even want to win the case against the opponents of equality except in a contest governed by the best traditions and highest standards of the scholarly vocation. They also know that this nation honors its own past and builds toward a noble future only as it struggles to redeem the promise which Lincoln saw as our unique duty and possiblity.

John H. Scharr
Kresge College
University of California
Santa Cruz
February 1983

ACKNOWLEDGEMENTS

The idea for this book developed in a project, Ethical Issues in Political Life, which was sponsored by the Division of Educational Affairs of the American Political Science Association and funded by the National Endowment for the Humanities. Our particular seminar, "Equality: Its Bearing on Justice and Liberty," was coordinated by John H. Schaar. We met at Stanford University in May and September, 1976, and have met many times since then in continuing discussion of the many dimensions of equality. Our thanks to the A.P.S.A.'s Division of Educational Affairs and to the National Endowment for the Humanities for providing the opportunity to initiate this collaboration. Mary Segers also wishes to acknowledge Rutgers University which granted her a Faculty Academic Study Program leave for one semester in 1977.

We are grateful to our families, friends and colleagues for their encouragement and assistance in completing this book. We especially thank each other for collegiality and friendship throughout.

J.C. F.
M.C. S.
M.C. T.
B.N. E.

Elusive Equality:
Liberalism, Affirmative Action, and Social Change in America

James C. Foster and Mary C. Segers
with
Mary C. Thornberry and Bette Novit Evans

To our children

INTRODUCTION

This book is several things. First, perhaps foremost, it is a book about equality in America. It was written to enable its authors, initially, and now its readers to better understand the social theory and practice of equality in this country. Since we were writing a textbook, our intention was not so much to break new ground as to synthesize many existing materials in a comprehensible, challenging way. We will have accomplished an important goal if our work enlarges your knowledge of the ideological and public policy aspects of equality, past and present, as well as engaging you to contemplate its future.

Becuase the future of equality—as a set of ideas and/or a program of action—affects us all, this book also advocates a point of view. We advocate basic changes in thought and in deed with regard to equality in America. We find many contemporary American values opposed to equality, and most present policies subversive of it. The book's substance embodies our views; its tone sometimes reflects our passion. We fully expect our readers to be engaged by what we say, debating with us over our particular interpretations, evaluation, and conclusions. A second goal we share is to stir up discussions about equality: agreeing with us is not as important as arguing with us over equality.

More than merely a discussion topic, equality is a central concern of American life. It is a condition many Americans take for granted. It is a goal to which many other Americans aspire. Equality evokes passion, prejudice, and polemics. Equality also gives rise to research, policy, and litigation. Even so, the concept of equality is not widely understood among Americans.

What has been going on with regard to equality in America and what ought to go on in the future are central topics of this book. Our analysis of and prescriptions about equality take the reader from British political philosophy prior to the founding of the American Republic up to current controversies over affirmative action. We seek to situate present political debates over equality in their historical context while illustrating the continuing relevance of our past. Section 1—"From Whence Have We Come?"—investigates the antecedents of American liberalism and examines how our liberal concepts of equality—what we term proprietary

3

equality—justified and explained the transformation of the democratic social conditions Alexis de Tocqueville observed in the America of the 1830s into Thorstein Veblen's late-nineteenth-century world of "pecuniary emulation."

Chapter 1 argues that our political tradition is proprietary with regard to equality in its defense of property and accumulation as ends in themselves. The chapter traces the origins of America's liberal political ideology to Thomas Hobbes and John Locke. We argue that equality, in liberal terms, is understood as equal individual ability (opportunity) to accumulate *different* amounts of property. Such proprietary equality teaches that equality exists to the extent that all have the chance to become unequal in material possessions. Such proprietary equality, we contend, is enmeshed in an economic system based upon unequal accumulation: capitalism. Since proprietary equality also teaches that who we are as a person is largely a consequence of what we own, it also results in inequalities of personal worth. Growing up in liberal America, we learn that being equal means getting ahead.

This dilemma exists both in Tocqueville's concern about the erosion of democracy in America and in Veblen's analysis of such erosion after the fact. The difference between them largely reflects the contrast between the incipient state of American capitalism when Tocqueville visited and its relative maturation by Veblen's time at the turn of the century. Tocqueville visited America during its salad days. Young, boisterous, energetic, innocent America was still a land of comparative social and economic equality—"comparative" because women, blacks, Native Americans, apprentices, and indentured servants lived lives of necessity and inferiority. Social and economic equality existed in terms of rough parities in status, wealth, and income among free white males. The irony of Tocqueville's observations is that he chronicled a set of circumstances that was in the process of vanishing. Even as he recorded it, the fortuitous American equality of conditions was being undermined enterprisingly by capitalists—a process legitimized by proprietary equality.

Chapter 2 charts the continuity of proprietary equality up to the modern era. In it we argue that perennial debates between so-called liberals (Democrats) and so-called conservatives (Republicans) are fundamentally beside the point with reference to equality because such debates seldom challenge liberal-capitalist orthodoxy. To a great extent, the difference between these two expressions of liberal-capitalist "consensus" has to do with how many Americans should be able to play the game of acquisition: liberals want to broaden participation; conservatives tend to restrict access. Both factions refrain from seriously scrutinizing the character and consequences of the game itself.

By the time Thorstein Veblen wrote, the equality of conditions which had so impressed Tocqueville had been profoundly changed. Individualism, materialism, and pursuit of private interests—tendencies recognized and pointed out by Tocqueville—had worked their consequences. The Gilded Age, to use Mark Twain's description, was in full bloom when Veblen wrote about conspicuous consumption as the American passion. By the turn of the last century, proprietary equality had effectively driven all challengers from the field of ideological battle, just as competitive capital emerging into monopoly capital held sway in the realm of production.

Chapter 2 examines two occurrences which pertained to equality at the turn of the century. In practice, disparities in income, wealth, and power grew to an extent unparalleled in American history. In the realm of jurisprudential theory, legal formalism—treating law in abstract terms—served to legitimate such inequality by treating real economic, political, and social conflicts as though they existed in a vacuum. While robber barons amassed vast empires, the Supreme Court waxed eloquent about the equality at law of two parties to a contract. In this fashion American public law assumed a dreamlike quality, as legal fictions took the place of economic realities.

What Veblen pointed out (to those who would listen) is that by 1900 Americans cared less about inequality than about being unequal. Pecuniary emulation, driven by the interests of capital and defended by proprietary equality, became the American Way of Life. When Sinclair Lewis wrote *Babbitt* (1922), art was imitating life. Given proprietary equality as an ideology, people who cannot compete effectively are seen, depending upon which aspect of liberalism one subscribes to, as either immoral or incompetent. Only the lazy or inept could fail to run the race like everyone else. Whether expressed in terms of Veblen's pecuniary emulation or Michael Lewis's "culture of inequality" (discussed at the close of Chapter 2), our dilemma in liberal-capitalist America remains the same: convinced that self-affirmation is a function of getting ahead, and living in a society where getting ahead is largely the result of social determinants, we nevertheless are sure we have only ourselves to praise or to blame for our lot in life.

The five chapters making up Section 2—"Where Are We Now?"—examine various aspects of the major attempt to achieve equality, not only in our time but in American history: affirmative action. Much maligned by conservatives, much invested with hope by liberals, affirmative action's history, implementation, and justification are analyzed in this section. As we write, affirmative action appears to be everybody's favorite program to hate. Reeling under charges that it has been ineffective, that it is discriminatory, that it does not (and cannot) differentiate between individuals or groups as beneficiaries (that it is a shotgun approach when a rifle is required), affirmative action seems jeopardized. We believe a stock taking is in order, particularly one that places affirmative action in an historical context. In the course of our examination it turns out that affirmative action does indeed affirm several important things.

First, and in some ways most significant, affirmative action affirms the commitment of American society to make its ideal of equality a reality. Conceived during the Johnson administration, subsequently supported and expanded through Democratic and Republican administrations alike, interpreted and upheld by courts at many levels of our judiciary including the Supreme Court, affirmative action is clear evidence that this country means what it says with regard to equal opportunity without regard to race, sex, color, creed, religion, or national origin. However narrowly proprietary our conception of equality may be (we will return to this matter below), affirmative action represents social progress, we submit, to the extent that it gives programmatic reality to otherwise hollow promises.

Second, affirmative action affirms the fundamental unity between the two factions of American liberalism. Differing marginally over how best to manage a capitalist economy, conservatives and liberals alike remain committed to the defense of that system of production. Conservatives reject affirmative action as excessive, ineffective government meddling in the market which, if left to its own "natural" devices, would bring women, blacks, and other disadvantaged into the fold. Liberals defend affirmative action (timidly these days) as the only means of providing economic opportunities to those discriminated against in this society. For us the notable thing is that, while either praised or damned, affirmative action rather than monopoly capitalism is the issue.

Third, affirmative action affirms the complexity of social problems. In recognizing the complexity of dealing with inequality in America, we are not subscribing to an au courant fatalism that conceives all social problems as intractable. Achieving equality will certainly involve tradeoffs. Moral choices are going to have to be examined, debated, and ultimately made. This does not mean, however, that we should throw in the towel collectively in lieu of the full-time pursuit of self-gratification. It seems to us that the days of relatively easy options—if you do not like your situation, move west, move into space, throw money at the problem—are over for Americans. We agree with historian William Appleman Williams when he wrote, "America has evaded nothing but the central issues." Central issues like equality are not easy issues. Equality must be confronted nevertheless.

Fourth, affirmative action affirms the exhaustion of American liberalism. Our examination of this policy shows, we believe, that affirmative action is insufficient to the achievement of genuine human equality in America. Thus, there is some truth to the charge of affirmative action's critics that the policy is ill conceived. Such opponents are particularly correct with regad to the limitations of the approach, but for the wrong reasons. Affirmative action illustrates the limitations of state and institutional attempts to create equality in a society where inequalities are primarily the result of structural characteristics inherent in an advanced capitalist economy. All the affirmative action programs we could muster would not significantly alter, for example, the great inequalities separating those few who own and control capital from the many who do not. By tying greater equality solely to expanding opportunities for individuals to accumulate more than others, American liberalism weds itself to the logic and the interests of capitalist expansion. Affirmative action epitomizes the exhaustion of a tradition that can no longer either legitimize or rectify existing inequalities.

Reflection upon what is required to enable us to escape this dilemma resulted in the two chapters which make up section 3: "Where Should We Go from Here?". The suggestions we make there are offered modestly and urgently. Without meaning to sound apocalyptic, we want to impart our sense that America stands at a crossroads. We are not talking about the extreme choice between, say, utopia or oblivion, to invoke R. Buckminster Fuller's phrase. America's choice is less sublime and more immediate. Our choice is the following: we can continue muddling through paying the price of growing numbers of unfulfilled, wasted lives attended by anger, resentment, and loss, or we can begin to restructure our society in ways which promise lower human costs and greater social strength. In a way, we have been standing still, marking time at this crossroads for quite a while. Our choice seems clearer now, our situation more poignant.

Our students seem to understand the dilemma we all face, at least implicitly. They are uncertain, dissatisfied, questioning. They are also highly skeptical, shortsighted, and acquisitive. Their lives embody our dilemma as Americans— and our choices—in a nutshell. We would like to think that, among the several things this book is, our work on equality is helpful in facilitating the difficult choices facing students and other readers.

SECTION ONE

From Whence Have We Come?

1

The Roots of American Notions About Equality

James C. Foster

> History was on a lark, out to tease men, not by shattering their
> dreams, but by fulfilling them with a sort of satiric accuracy.
> **Lewis Hartz**
> *The Liberal Tradition in America*

The dominant political ideology in the United States is liberalism. Liberalism functions as a cultural blueprint,[1] an integrated set of symbols which explain and justify the collective political goals we share and actions we pursue. With reference to equality, liberalism colors our perceptions both of existing problems and potential solutions. It is important to understand that as an ideology liberalism provides Americans with necessary meanings while also limiting our vision. If we are going to be able to perceive equality from an expanded point of view, it is necessary, first, to realize that liberalism is but one among several perspectives and, second, to comprehend fully the origins and consequences of the view of equality dominating our culture. Once these tasks have been accomplished, it will be possible to consider other ways of thinking about equality.

For purposes of understanding the roots of American notions about equality, the ideas which influenced the development of liberalism are of especial importance. In particular, we need to examine the role played by the works of Thomas Hobbes (1588-1679) and John Locke (1632-1704) in the fertile soil of American circumstances. The cultural chemistry between the work of these two British philosophers and the founding of a new nation on the vast North American continent resulted in an enduring ideological bond, a bond which exists to this day. In an almost uncanny way American political culture continues to reproduce Hobbes's and Locke's political theories. This situation is noted in Lewis Hartz's influential analysis of Lockean liberalism in America and is the reason he is quoted at the head of this chapter. In the United States, early liberal political philosophy became a kind of self-evident truth, an ongoing self-fulfilling prophecy. Locke may have had an inkling of this situation when he wrote, "In the beginning all the world was America, and no more so than that is now...."[2]

Liberalism in America may be traced in part to the political philosophies of these two seventeenth-century Englishmen. In particular, there are strong theoretical affinities between the ideas of Locke and Hobbes on equality, and the liberal conceptions of equality prevalent in our society. Before examining Hobbes's and Locke's theories as they bear upon equality, however, we need to establish the primacy of Hobbes and Locke as our ideological progenitors. There are two preliminary matters to be considered. First is the explicit claim that American liberalism can be attributed primarily to Hobbes and Locke. Second is the implicit argument that Hobbes and Locke share more than they do not. Ultimately, the two points are related.

The identification of John Locke as a basic source of American political ideas is commonplace. Undoubtedly, Montesquieu, Adam Smith, James Harrington, John Stuart Mill, and others[3] have had an impact upon American political theory and practice. Nevertheless, as Hartz demonstrates in his classic *The Liberal Tradition in America,* "The American community is a liberal community."[4] What Hartz meant by "liberal" is Lockean. We want to argue that Hartz is partially correct. He is correct in identifying the American political tradition as predominantly liberal. He incorrectly attributes that liberalism *solely* to Locke, neglecting Hobbes and the context of capitalism in which liberalism was forged.

If casting John Locke in a basic role is conventional, perceiving Thomas Hobbes as sharing that role generally is not. If anything, Hobbes is seen typically as laying theoretical foundations for an illiberal society. Hobbes's *Leviathan* is widely interpreted as providing the justification for authoritarian government, one to which people surrender their rights in return for security from the consequences of innate human greed. Locke's *Second Treatise,* on the other hand, is viewed as laying the basis for liberal democracy grounded in natural law and committed to preserving human rights. The problem with this interpretation is not that it misreads Hobbes's argument. The problem arises when, in tracing the origins of American political ideology, Hobbes is neglected and Locke is understood as being antithetical to Hobbes.

To be sure, Hobbes's political philosophy is neither flattering to human nature nor hospitable to self-government among humans. Hobbes was candid about the sorts of personal aspirations, values, and interpersonal relations characteristic of an acquisitive society. Hobbes generalized about human beings in these terms: "In the first place, I put for a general inclination of all mankind, a perpetual and restless desire for power after power, that ceaseth only in death. And the cause of this is...because he cannot assure the power and means to live well, which he hath present, without the acquisition of more."[5] Whether or not Hobbes's sweeping characterization applies to all humans under all circumstances, we submit it is an apt description of Americans past and present. There is no small irony in the fact that Americans, just like Hobbes's contemporaries, reject the candor of his descriptions while vigorously engaging in activities which give rise to them. Americans derive comfort from the Lockean phrases of our Declaration of Independence and the Bill of Rights while pursuing power under the legal umbrella of our more Hobbesian Constitution.[6]

Another way of putting this is to say that American politics is characterized by

Lockean forms and Hobbesian substance. By this we mean that the congenial appearance of American liberalism, associated with civil liberties, government by consent, and the rule of law, is consistently eclipsed by the reality of oppression evidenced in hierarchical relations and bureaucratic unaccountability, in racism and sexism, and in great disparities in wealth and power in American society. Political rights in such a system are undermined by social and economic inequalities. Hobbesian competition in the private sector vitiates political rights in the public sector. The point is that the Lockean character of American liberal politics is overshadowed by the Hobbesian competitive character of much of our commercial life. The resultant mix is the ideology of liberal-capitalism. No one expressed this mix better than Martin Diamond. "It is tempting to suggest," Diamond wrote, "that if America is a 'Lockean' nation, as is so often asserted, it is true in the very precise sense that Locke's 'comfortable preservation' displaces the harshness of the Hobbesian view, while not repudiating that view in general."[7] As Diamond well understood, American politics embodies Lockean solutions to Hobbesian problems.

While Hobbes and Locke reach different conclusions concerning political institutions, they share similar philosophical assumptions about human nature and the nature of society. These assumptions depict human beings as primarily acquisitive, self-interested individuals who are related in society in an abstract, rational manner. Since this conception of human nature is perhaps an apt description of Americans, we must examine further how the American ideology of liberalism can be traced to Hobbes and Locke.

The political philosophies of Thomas Hobbes and John Locke were the reflections of two brilliant men upon the circumstances in which they lived. Their time was ripe for a reformulation of social theory, a reformulation that would incorporate the multifarious changes European society had undergone in the course of emerging from the medieval period. The period in which Hobbes and Locke wrote saw England in the throes of shedding the remnants of feudalism and emerging into the era of merchant (bourgeois) capitalism. The 116 years spanned by Hobbes's and Locke's collective lifetimes were tumultuous and full of change. The new social theories spawned during this period laid the groundwork for American political thinking.

Leviathan and *The Second Treatise of Civil Government* reflect the milieu which gave them birth. During the time these works were written, equality came to be understood in a manner compatible with what C.B. Macpherson has characterized as the prevailing ethos of seventeenth-century England, namely, possessive individualism.[8] According to Macpherson, "Seventeenth-century individualism contained [a] central difficulty, which lay in its possessive quality. Its possessive quality is found in its conception of the individual as essentially the proprietor of his own person or capacities, owing nothing to society for them."[9] This view of human nature and society which emphasized possessive individualism incorporated the following elements: (1) individual independence from the will of others; (2) freedom from relations with others, except for self-interested relations voluntarily contracted; (3) individual proprietorship of person and capacities; (4) individual ability to sell one's labor capacity; (5) a conception of society as a series of market relations; (6) restrictions upon individual freedom only to the extent necessary to secure the same freedom for others; and (7) a conception of the end of government as protection of the individual's person and property.[10]

For Macpherson, an important change occurring in seventeenth-century English thought was the reduction of human nature to that of *Homo economicus.* Human beings were shorn of all their complexity. All that was left of the human soul, using the idiom of classical Greek philosophers, were the appetitive and calculative aspects. Trucking and bartering, to this proprietary creature, comprised the whole of life. The model of human nature underlying this society was most explicitly articulated in Hobbes's work. In the thirteenth chapter of *Leviathan,* for example, Hobbes wrote:

In the nature of man, we find three principle causes of quarrel. First, competition; secondly, diffidence; thirdly glory. The first, maketh men invade for gain; the second, for safety; and the third, for reputation. The first use violence, to make themselves masters of other men's persons, wives, children, and cattle; the second, to defend them; the third, for trifles, as a word, a smile, a different opinion, and any other sign of undervalue, either direct in their persons, or by reflection in their kindred, their friends, their nation, their profession, or their name.[11]

Locke succeeded in moderating the tone of Hobbes's model of human nature. His modifications, according to Macpherson, did not essentially alter the substance of Hobbes's view but rendered it more palatable to the men of property who ruled English society, by couching possessive individualism in terms of reason and rights. Of the state of nature, over against Hobbes's state of war, Locke wrote: "The State of Nature has a Law of Nature to govern it, which obliges every one: And Reason, which is that Law, teaches all Mankind, who will but consult it, *that being all equal* and independent, no one ought to harm another in his Life, Health, Liberty, or Possessions."[12]

Whether striving after power or endowed with certain rights, human beings as described by Hobbes and Locke are creatures of property. Men in Locke's state of nature were perhaps more "civilized" than those in Hobbes's prepolitical state, but they were no less acquisitive. Locke's justification for the founding of civil society illustrates this:

The only way whereby any one divests himself of his Natural Liberty, and puts on the bonds of Civil Society is by agreeing with other Men to joyn and unite into a Community, for their comfortable, safe, and peaceable living one amongst another, in a secure Enjoyment of their Properties, and a greater Security against any that are not of it.[13]

As Macpherson points out, Locke's work is the more subtle and complex of the two. What the *Second Treatise* lacks in clarity it gains in its ability to avoid the harshness of *Leviathan.* Hobbes forged the substance of possessive individualism; Locke tempered it. Together they constituted the political theory of an emerging capitalist order.

How does possessive individualism pertain to equality? In what way does it give rise to what we term *proprietary equality,* which is equality among individual competitors in an acquisitive society? What are the differences of emphasis distinguishing Hobbes from Locke? We turn now to consider these important questions.

One must extrapolate the substance of proprietary equality from the theory of possessive individualism. As we have seen, possessive individualism centers on acquisition as a means toward the fundamental goal of human beings in bourgeois society: to be unencumbered. What this amounts to is owning enough so that one's independence from the will(s) of others is maximized. In other words, the ultimate end is negative sort of freedom—to be left alone. Equality, given these assumptions, is effectively either an illusion or an apology. For proprietary equality is a contradiction with two variations: either it justifies unequal results by means of equal beginnings, or it conceals substantive inequality behind equal formal rights. Proprietary equality thereby inevitably furthers *in*equality.

This is not to suggest that equality was not taken seriously by Hobbes and Locke. As social contract theorists who held that political society is not naturally ordained but is instituted by humans through voluntary agreement or compact, they had to assume that human beings were created equal. Contract theory assumes—indeed must assume—initial equality among human beings in a prepolitical situation or "state of nature." For it makes no sense to speak of a contract between unequal parties. Moreover, a contract between unequals simply would not work; it would degenerate rapidly into a might-makes-right situation in which political arrangements would automatically reflect basic inequalities of power. Thus, both logical and practical necessity led Hobbes and Locke to posit human equality.

The passages in which Hobbes spoke of equality are rather eloquent. Hobbes regarded humans as naturally equal in physical strength and in mental ability:

Nature has made men so equal in the faculties of body and mind; as that though there be found one man sometimes manifestly stronger in body or of quicker mind than another, yet, when all is reckoned together, the difference between man and man is not so considerable as that one man can thereupon claim to himself any benefit to which another may not pretend as well as he. For as to the strength of body, the weakest has strength enough to kill the strongest.... And as to the faculties of the mind...I find yet a greater equality among men than that of strength. For prudence is but experience, which equal time equally bestows on all men in those things they equally apply themselves to. That which may perhaps make such equality incredible is but a vain conceit of one's own wisdom, which almost all men think they have in a greater degree than the vulgar—that is, than all men but themselves and a few others.[14]

To Hobbes this rough parity among human beings was an empirical description of the way people actually are at birth. The social inequalities we see around us are artificial hierarchies created by a world that wishes to have ranks. Yet, in case one might doubt Hobbes's assumption of natural equality, witness how he made egalitarian attitudes a moral obligation in his civil society:

The question who is the better man has no place in the condition of mere nature, where...all men are equal. The inequality that now is has been introduced by the laws civil...If nature therefore have made men equal, that equality is to be acknowledged; or if nature have made men unequal, yet because men that think themselves equal will not enter into conditions of peace but upon equal terms, such equality must be admitted. And therefore for the ninth law of nature, I put this: *that every man acknowledge another for his equal by nature*. The breach of this precept is pride.[15]

Having first argued that human beings are *in fact* natural equals, Hobbes later argued that people *should regard* one another as equals. This jump from a statement of fact to a statement of value has always been of interest to those who study Hobbes. Not only does it raise the perennial philosophical issue of the is/ought or fact/value dichotomy, it also indicates that Hobbes saw the need in political society of reinforcing otherwise fragile egalitrian norms. The problem for Hobbes is simple: if humans are natural equals, why do they have a duty to regard one another as equals in political society? Will they not simply continue to regard each other as peers?

The answer to this apparent problem is found in Hobbes's conception of human beings as infinitely acquisitive and in his description of the state of nature. The fact that people are equals in the state of nature puts them on a collision course with one another. For, primarily, humans are equally grasping:

From this equality of ability arises equality of hope in the attaining of our ends. And therefore if any two men desire the same thing, which nevertheless they cannot both enjoy, they become enemies; and in the way to their end, which is principally their own conservation, and sometimes their delectation only, endeavor to destroy or subdue one another.[16]

The result of this behavior is a situation Hobbes describes as the war of all against all. The only way out of such a barbarous condition is for free and equal individuals to agree to create an inequality of civil power. Thus, through the social contract they concentrate political power in the hands of an absolute sovereign who will overawe them, keep them in fear of its power, and thereby create civil order. In this manner Hobbes's initial natural equality leads inexorably to "artificial" political and social inequalities. In this fashion regarding others as peers becomes a duty that one ought to do rather than something one does naturally.

In sum, Hobbes's egalitariansim is limited. Rousseau's criticism of Hobbes on this point is well taken.[17] The development of civil society leads humans away from a prepolitical situation of natural equality into a society marked by artificial yet powerful inequalities. In the end, Hobbes justifies unequal results by appealing to equal beginnings.

"Hobbes," remarks Macpherson, "caught both the freedom and the compulsion of possessive market society." The resulting portrait of life is as unappealing as it is undisguised. Macpherson's comment could just as well be applied to the conception of equality in Hobbes's work. An equal opportunity to do each other bodily harm, resting on equal vulnerability and equally voracious appetites, renders all people equally fearful for their lives. This is the gist of perhaps the most often quoted passage from *Leviathan:*

Whatsoever therefore is consequent to a time of war, where every man is enemy to every man; the same is consequent to the time, wherein men live without other security, than what their own strength, and their own invention shall furnish them withal. In such condition, there is no place for industry; because the fruit thereof is uncertain; and consequently no culture of the earth; no navigation, nor use of the commodities that may be imported by sea; no commodious building; no instruments of moving and removing, such things as require much force; no knowledge of the face of the earth; no account of time; no arts; no letters; no society; and which is worst of all, continual fear, and danger of violent death; and the life of man, solitary, poor, nasty, brutish, and short.[18]

Of course, it should be pointed out that Hobbes is describing here the human condition as he understood it outside protections offered by his authoritarian civil society. Nevertheless, while Hobbes's *Leviathan* quelled the state of war, it merely tamed and channeled acquisitive human appetites. It did not seek to change that which it assumed unchanging.

Like Hobbes, Locke as a contract theorist had to assume initial equality among human beings in a prepolitical state of nature. However, whereas Hobbes offers an elaborate argument justifying his belief in natural equality, Locke simply posits equality as a self-evident truth. Describing "the state all men are naturally in," Locke writes that it is a state of freedom and

a state also of equality, wherein all the power and jurisdiction is reciprocal, no one having more than another; there being nothing more evident than that creatures of the same species and rank, promiscuosly born to all the same advantages of nature and the use of the same faculties, should also be equal one amongst another without subordination or subjection.[19]

In contrast to Hobbes, Locke seems more inclined to admit innate differences among humans. While Hobbes argues for a rough physical and mental parity among people, Locke's initial equality is compatible with many differences. In the end, natural equality for Locke seems to mean that in a state of nature which, by definition, is devoid of government, no one is under the authority of anyone else; all persons are equally free and independent:

Though I have said above that all men by nature are equal, I cannot be supposed to understand all sorts of equality. Age or virtue may given men a just precedence; excellence of parts and merit may place others above the common level: birth may subject some, and alliance or benefits others, to pay an observance to those whom nature, gratitude, or other respects may have made it due; and yet all this consists with the equality which all men are in, in respect of jurisdiction or dominion one over another, which was the equality I there spoke of as proper to the business in hand, being that equal right that every man has to his natural freedom, without being subjected to the will or authority of any other man.[20]

The natural rights to life, liberty, and property which humans possess in Locke's state of nature are possessed equally by all. However, as we shall see, the actual realization of these equal human rights varies according to differences in political power, social class, and economic wealth.

In addition to Locke's positing of a self-evident natural equality and an equal sharing of natural rights, Locke is a proponent of constitutional or limited government who emphasized the necessity for the rule of law. Locke is therefore committed to legal equality. Equality before the law means that all citizens come under the aegis of the law and that courts must decide cases according to what has been called the rule of justice[21] or the principle of formal equality: treat like cases alike.[22] To Locke the rule of law meant that every civilized community had to adjudicate disputes through appeals to "settled standing rules, indifferent and the same to all parties."[23] Judges and administrators had a duty to treat similar cases in similar ways, evenly and impartially, with no trace of preference or favoritism. In law and administration, justice meant neutral, impartial, nonpreferential, equal treatment.

Of course, the principle that like cases should be treated alike is a formal norm since it does not indicate how cases should be treated or in what respects cases are to be regarded as similar. Moreover, this principle of formal equality before the law seems quite compatible with great inequality and with great injustice. As Chaim Perelman has noted, the principle of treating like cases alike is quite compatible with a slave owner's treating all his slaves equally—equally harshly.[24]

As a liberal, then, Locke posited an initial natural equality and held that all individuals equally have certain natural rights. As a constitutionalist, Locke espoused limited government, separation of powers, the rule of law, and a commitment to equality before the law. It should be clear, however, that equality in Locke's theory is largely formal and procedural. In those instances when it is substantive, equality is an instrumental value of subsidiary importance, a means to other more important ends such as freedom and independence.

Two factors serve to undermine and dilute Locke's commitment to equality. First, Locke is typical of his time in that he is not a democrat. We do not find in the *Second Treatise* any argument for political equality; there is little if any discussion of universal suffrage, equal access to government, or equal opportunity to stand for election. On the contrary, numerous passages in Locke suggest his acceptance and endorsement of the political implications of the highly structured class society that was seventeenth-century England.[25]

Second, Locke's passages on property acquisition indicate how much he was influenced by the developing capitalism of his time. As Macpherson states, "In the last analysis it was Locke's comprehension of his own society that was ambiguous and contradictory. It could scarcely have been otherwise. It reflected accurately enough the ambivalence of an emerging bourgeois society which demanded formal equality but required substantive inequality of rights."[26] Formal equality and substantive inequality: Locke's position exemplifies the contradiction between what political scientist Murray Edelman calls symbolic and concrete politics.[27] More specifically, in the American context, it exemplifies the contradiction between procedural democracy and monopoly capitalism.

Locke's discussion of property, given to all in common and also possessed differentially, provides a good illustration of this paradox. Locke wrote, on the one hand:

Whether we consider natural Reason, which tells us, that Men, being once born, have a right to their Preservation, and consequently to Meat and Drink, and such other things, as Nature affords for their Subsistence: Or Revelation, which gives us an account of those Grants God made of the World to Adam, and to Noah, and his Sons, 'tis very clear, that

God, as King David says, Psal. CXV. xvi. has given the Earth to the Children of Men, given it to Mankind in common.

Coming then to his purpose, Locke continued:

> But this being supposed, it seems to some a very great difficulty, how any one should ever come to have a Property in any thing: I will not content my self to answer.... But I shall endeavor to shew, how Men might come to have a property in several parts of that which God gave to Mankind in common, and that without any express Compact of all the Commoners.[28]

Locke's accomplishment was to reconcile theoretical commitment to equality with practical inequality. Politically, he managed to square a circle. The key to his achievement, which has been crucial to continued legitimacy of liberal-capitalism, is Locke's discussion of money. His argument proceeds in this manner: God, in giving property to all mankind in common, intended for that property to be used; that it not lie fallow, so to speak. Individuals appropriate property from the common holdings through their labor, that is, by making use of God-given, common property. In this way what was common becomes exclusively private so long, as Locke put it, as "there is enough, and as good left in common for others."[29] Locke thereby attached two stipulations to individual appropriation: that no single person take more than can be used before it spoils, and take no more than will leave enough for others. Locke summarized his argument up to this point in this way: "So that God, by commanding to subdue, gave Authority so far to appropriate. And the Condition of Human Life, which requires Labour and Materials to work on, necessarily introduces private Possessions."

On the page following this statement Locke first makes mention of money. Shortly thereafter he fashioned his justification for unequal appropriation. Money, being durable, provided human beings with the ability to increase their property beyond what they could use.

> If [an individual] would give us Nuts for a piece of Metal, pleased with its colour; or exchanged his Sheep for Shells, or Wool for a sparkling Pebble or a Diamond, and keep those by him all his life, *he invaded not the Right of others,* he might heap up as much of these durable things as he pleased; the exceeding of the bounds of his just Property not lying in the largeness of his Possession, but the perishing of any thing uselessly in it.... And thus came in the use of Money.[30]

In section 50 of his chapter on property, Locke summarized his argument.

> Since Gold and Silver, being little useful to the Life of Man in proportion to Food, Rayment, and Carriage, has its value only from the consent of Men, whereof Labour yet makes, in great part, the measure, it is plain, that *Men have agreed to disproportionate and unequal Possession of the Earth,* they having by a tacit and voluntary consent found out a way, how a man may fairly possess more land than he himself can use the product of, by receiving in exchange for the overplus, Gold and Silver, which may be hoarded up without injury to any one, these metalls not spoiling or decaying in the hands of the possessor.[31]

Thus was capitalist production, production for exchange and not for use, justified by couching it in terms of the acquisition of money. Thus, too, was born the contradiction between formal equality and substantive inequality inherent in liberal-capitalist American theory and practice. Locke's contribution to proprietary equality was to legitimize the sort of accumulation which ensures unequal wealth and power to the few and equal dependence to the many. As Macpherson writes, "Locke could not have been conscious that the individuality he championed was at the same time a denial of individuality.... The contradiction was there, but it was impossible for [him] to recognize it, let alone to resolve it."[32]

Figure 1 summarizes the ground covered in this chapter. It condenses this discussion of proprietary equality and relates it to the dominant American political tradition. By examining the lineage traced there, it is possible to more clearly understand from whence American notions of equality derive. Figure 1 additionally serves as a useful introduction to the analysis contained in the following chapter. There it will be discovered (not surprisingly) that the Hobbesian and Lockean emphases within liberalism define the character of American political thought and practice. In particular it will be seen that Americans have consistently defined equality in proprietary terms, thereby effectively precluding the realization of a genuinely egalitarian society in the United States.

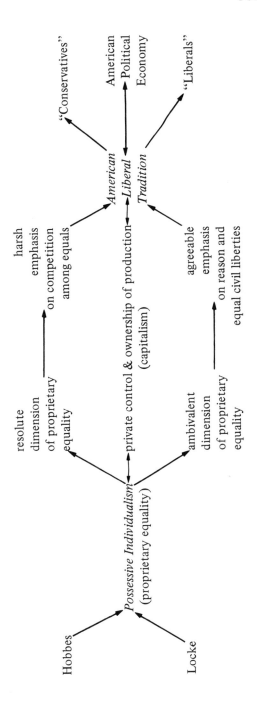

FIGURE 1
LINEAGE OF AMERICAN NOTIONS OF EQUALITY

2

The Fundamental Continuity
of Proprietary Equality in America

James C. Foster

The passions that agitate the Americans most deeply are not their political, but their commercial passions; or rather, they introduce the habits of business into their political life.

Alexis de Tocqueville
Democracy in America

[America] has been run on the assumption that the greatest value of all is liberty, which gives people the freedom to "do their own thing," particularly in making money, regardless of how much this freedom deprives others of the same liberty—or of a decent standard of living.

Herbert J. Gans
More Equality

American history chronicles the ascendancy of liberalism. More precisely, it records the unabated triumph of that ideology and the capitalist material conditions supporting it. As such, American history also records the dominance of proprietary equality—that complex, contradictory notion of two variations on one theme: possessive individualism. In light of the previous chapter it should be clear that proprietary equality unites a "realistic" acceptance of inequality based upon the equality of human avarice (Hobbes) with an "idealistic" blindness to inequality resulting from formally equal rights (Locke). These two dimensions of liberal-capitalism coexist in ways which, if seldom harmonious, are functionally complementary. Both serve to legitimate inequality in America by means of powerful symbols. Together they define the meaning of equality to most Americans, thereby determining American practices.

This chapter traces the manifestations of proprietary equality from The Founding to contemporary times. Its primary thesis is that although apparently much has changed about the politics of equality in America—names, specific issues, alignments—the values underpinning our notions of equality have remained remarkably consistent. In short, this chapter deals with fundamental continuity which presents an ephemeral face.

Our odyssey begins prior to The Founding in 1789. Something important happened on the way to Philadelphia and the Constitution: American political sentiments began to shift in significant ways. One way to characterize this changed emphasis is to say that American attachment to active self-government and ongoing participation in political matters gave way, by and large, to overriding commitment to acquisition. Generally, the *public* Spirit of '76 was eroded by the *private* pursuit of happiness. Having fought and won their revolt against Britain, Americans turned their collective sights away from active involvement in the body politic and toward the prospects of individual enrichment. Hector St. John de Crevecoeur, patriot and acute observer of American ways, predicted this change and feared it when he wrote in 1782, "The man will get the better of the citizen...his political maxims will vanish." Crevecoeur perhaps would have been more precise had he noted that American political maxims did not vanish; individual consumption simply came to define them.[1]

America of the revolutionary period was a country infected with self-conscious nationhood. The prevailing sentiments were public-spiritedness and community. Sectional and other rivalries were transcended in the movement toward the goal of independence. Americans joined together in common cause. Men and women made great personal sacrifices to advance independence—something which, to be sure, benefited them individually, yet not them alone. To make this argument is not to romanticize what was in many ways a very pragmatic revolt. Nevertheless, there is no denying the sense of public involvement abroad in America, a feeling of commitment beyond one's immediate advancement. Animating the revolutionary generation was a social, in contrast to an egoistic, esprit. This is the unmistakable meaning of the words closing our Declaration of Independence: "And for the support of this Declaration, with firm reliance on the protection of divine Providence, we mutually pledge to each other our Lives, our Fortunes and our Sacred Honor." If the sentiment expressed by these words is not exactly altruism, neither is it narcissism.

These fleeting public sentiments and commitments brought with them large rewards as well as large responsibilities. Americans of this period understood that, whatever the constraints of civic virtue, self-rule entailed important advantages. "The point," wrote the late Hannah Arendt, "is that Americans knew that public freedom consisted in having a share in public business, and that the activities connected with this business by no means constituted a burden but gave those who discharged them in public a feeling of happiness they could acquire nowhere else."[2] This assessment applies most clearly to the leaders, one might say the elites, of the American Revolution. Nevertheless, such public happiness—the sense of accomplishment and fulfillment which comes with active participation in the affairs of one's community—was not an exclusive experience.

Central to understanding the generality of public participation during the revolutionary period is the concept of republicanism. As the term was used at the time, republicanism stood for commitment to self-government. Widespread in its adherents, republicanism was the abiding passion of the time. As historian Gordon S. Wood writes, "No phrase except 'liberty' was evoked more often by the Revolutionaries than 'the public good.' This phrase expressed the colonists' deepest hatreds of the old order and their most visionary hopes for the new."[3] Commitment to the public good and republicanism went hand in hand. In order to preserve the latter, one had to be committed to the former. Wood states: "The sacrifice of individual interests to the greater good of the whole formed the essence of republicanism and comprehended for Americans the idealistic goal of the revolution. From this goal flowed all of the American's exhortatory literature and all that made their ideology truly revolutionary."[4]

In America, sad to say, this pervasive attachment to the commonweal has been eclipsed by a profound attachment to the private pursuit of accumulation. The revolutionary spirit of which Wood speaks thus has been submerged among antisocial tendencies which have professionalized politics and elevated pecuniary emulation[5] to a national pastime. Arendt made the point this way: "Paradoxical as it may sound, it was in fact under the impact of the Revolution that the revolutionary spirit in this country began to wither away, and it was the Constitution itself, this greatest achievement of the American people, which eventually cheated them of their proudest possession."[6]

The Constitution effectively shrank the public realm—the realm in which people can involve themselves in politics—to government and voting. It erected formal democratic procedures in the place of substantive democracy. With regard to their revolutionary goals, Americans won the battle but lost the war. Arendt's penetrating analysis of how America lost the treasure of its revolutionary tradition merits citation at some length:

The failure of post-revolutionary thought to remember the revolutionary spirit and to understand it conceptually was preceded by the failure of the revolution to provide it with a lasting institution.... In this republic, as it presently turned out, there was no space reserved, no room left for the exercise of precisely those qualities which had been instrumental in building it.... The perplexity was very simple and, stated in logical terms, it seemed unresolvable: if foundation was the aim and the end of revolution, then the revolutionary spirit was not merely the spirit of beginning something new but of starting something permanent and enduring; a lasting institution, embodying this spirit and encouraging it to new achievements, would be self-defeating. From which it unfortunately seems to follow that nothing threatens the very achievements of revolution more dangerously and more acutely than the spirit which has brought them about. Should freedom, in its most exalted sense as freedom to act, be the price to be paid for foundation? This perplexity, namely that the principle of public freedom and public happiness without which no revolution would ever have come to pass should remain the privilege of the generation of the founders...has haunted all revolutionary thinking ever since.[7]

A basic consequence of this situation is that the American notion of equality, always ambiguous in character, has been shorn of connotations pertaining to political participation, save that of voting, and suffused instead with private, proprietary meanings. Equality in America no longer entails active involvement in self-government among a society of peers. On the contrary, "equality" has become a counterrevolutionary apology for antipolitical activities giving rise to invidious disparities among Americans. Wood describes how politics changed between 1776, when it was characterized by public-spiritedness, and 1787, when it came to embody proprietary equality. Politics in the latter society, Wood notes,

...could no longer be simply described as a contest between rulers and people, between institutionalized orders of the society. The political struggles would in fact be among the people themselves, among all the various groups and individuals *seeking to create inequality out of their equality* by gaining control of a government divested of its former identity with the society.[8]

By the Constitutional Convention in Philadelphia, then, Americans had traveled some distance from their revolutionary heritage. Hobbes's and Locke's possessive individualism had come to the fore. Public equality was being abandoned in lieu of proprietary equality.

Into this situation, the American world of the early 1800s, came Alexis de Tocqueville. Ostensibly he came to study American prison conditions. In fact, convinced that equality of condition (what he termed democracy) was the singular, unavoidable wave of the future, Tocqueville came to study the "one country in the world where the great social revolution that I am speaking of seems to have nearly reached its natural limits."[9] His arrival was very timely. Right before Tocqueville's perceptive eyes Americans were busily creating the "inequality out of their equality" which Gordon Wood spoke of above. Of the many insights contained in Tocqueville's unsurpassed reflections, three in particular are germane to our inquiry here: (1) the source and nature of equality in America; (2) the manifestations of the process at work which would eventually undermine that equality; and (3) the unanimity among Americans with regard to their political values and goals (the problem of the "tyranny of the majority"). Underlying all three observations is a set of circumstances central to what we conceive of as proprietary equality: Americans generally take equality, of a sort, for granted and spend their energies seeking to become materially unequal. Tocqueville was thus a firsthand observer of how the philosophical worlds of Hobbes and Locke, discussed in the previous chapter, came to life in America.

It would not be inaccurate to say that Tocqueville perceived democracy (equality) in America as owing its existence at least as much to luck as to the special qualities of its inhabitants. Although he did not speak in terms of luck, Tocqueville, for example, said of our successful colonial revolt:

All ages have furnished the spectacle of a people struggling with energy to win its independence; and the efforts of the Americans in throwing off the English yoke have been considerably exaggerated. Separated from their enemies by three thousand miles of ocean, and backed by a powerful ally, the United States owed their victory much more to their geographical position than to the valor of their armies or the patriotism of their citizens.[10]

At another point he commented "A thousand circumstances independent of the will of man facilitate the maintenance of a democratic republic in the United States.... The Americans had the chances of birth in their favor...."[11]

According to Tocqueville, then, good fortune was the basic source of equality in America. For Locke, as we have seen, in the beginning (in the state of nature) all the world was America. Now we understand that, for Tocqueville, *from its beginning* America was a democratic (equal) society: "The great advantage of the Americans is that they have arrived at a state of democracy without having to endure a democratic revolution, and that *they are born equal instead of becoming so.*[12]

The significance of these circumstances surrounding our founding can hardly be overstated. Never having known any other conditions such as feudalism, and having inherited, so to speak, a society in which the social question, to use Hannah Arendt's term,[13] by dint of luck or good fortune had never been raised, Americans typically assume that equality is an irreversible fact of life. To be born an American is to be equal: equally empowered to pursue one's desires (Hobbes) and equally possessed of rights (Locked). As a result, equality is taken for granted as an innate fact of life rather than as an achieved condition to be placed on this society's agenda.

What was the nature of equality in America when Tocqueville visited? How does its nature relate to proprietary equality? To begin with, equality in America in the early decades of the nineteenth century was a matter of roughly similar material conditions. Americans—excluding, of course, most women, blacks, Native Americans, and indentured servants, all of whom collectively comprised a very sizable majority—lived comfortable lives. Ours was a nation of yeoman farmers, craftsmen, small merchants, traders, and bankers. To be sure, wealth was concentrated in the hands of entrepreneurs and financiers in the Northeast and land-owners of the South, but most white male Americans were self-employed. Relative equality of opportunity and of rights had substantive meaning. Hobbes's and Locke's visions seemed to be confirmed in American everyday life.

Nonetheless, Tocqueville foresaw in the character of American equality—proprietary equality—the seeds of its own undoing. These traits took the form of two abiding American passions about with the Frenchman worried: individualism and materialism. Early on, in chapter 5 of his first volume, Tocqueville spoke of the depth of American individualism in terms which should remind the reader of our discussion of possessive individualism in the previous chapter. Of the American, Tocqueville wrote:

He is free, and responsible to God alone, for all that concerns himself. Hence arises the maxim, that everyone is the best and sole judge of his own private interest, and that society has no right to control a man's actions unless they are prejudicial to the common weal or unless the common weal demands his help. This doctrine is universally admitted in the United States.[14]

According to Tocqueville, the danger in this maxim is that it would give rise to antisocial striving and grasping, thereby jeopardizing the very equality which the doctrine assumed. Tocqueville understood this process, as he demonstrated in his chapter "Of Individualism in Democratic Countries":

Selfishness blights the germ of all virtue; individualism, at first, only saps the virtues of public life; but in the long run it attacks and destroys all others and is at length absorbed in downright selfishness. Selfishness is a vice as old as the world, which does not belong to one form of society more than to another; individualism is of democratic origin, and it threatens to spread in the same ratio as the equality of condition.[15]

Tocqueville concluded this chapter,

"Thus not only does democracy make every man forget his ancestors, but it hides his descendants and separates his contemporaries from him; it throws him back forever upon himself alone and threatens in the end to confine him entirely within the solitude of his own heart."[16]

At this point we need to make clear one central disagreement between our analysis of proprietary equality and Tocqueville's study of equality in America. Although Tocqueville accurately analyzed the process through which equality was eroded, he misdiagnosed the source of this process, incorrectly attributing individualism to "the equality of condition" Americans had inherited rather than to the internal dynamics of a developing capatalist society. Tocqueville blamed equality for many social evils when he should have faulted, as we do, capitalism. In this criticism we are not alone. Writing in the introduction to Tocqueville's second volume, John Stuart Mill called Tocqueville to task for having termed a cause what was in fact an effect: "M. de Tocqueville then has, at least apparently, confounded the effects of Democracy with the effects of Civilization. He has bound up in one abstract idea the whole of the tendencies of modern commercial society, and given them one name—Democracy.[17]

Considering the example of the French of lower Canada, Mill wrote:

So far is it, from being admissable, that mere equality of conditions is the mainspring of those moral and social phenomena which M. de Tocqueville has characterised, that when some unusual chance exhibits to us equality of conditions by itself, severed from that commercial state of society and that progress of industry of which it is the natural concomitant, it produces few or none of the moral effects ascribed to it. . . . We by no means deny, that where the other circumstances which determine these effects exist, equality of conditions has a very perceptible effect in corroborating them. . . . But that it is the exclusive or even the principal cause, we think the example of Canada goes far to disprove.[18]

Following an examination of the additional example of Great Britian where, *without* equality of conditions but with "the rapid growth of industry and wealth" "in nearly all the moral and intellectual features of American society, as represented by M. de Tocqueville," Great Britain resembles America, Mill concluded, "The defects which M. de Tocqueville points out in the American, and which we see in the modern English mind, are the ordinary ones of a commercial class."[19]

Despite his error in attributing to equality what is more accurately ascribed to capitalism, we believe that Tocqueville's description of its manifestations is excellent. With regard to materialism Tocqueville wrote:

> It is strange to see with what feverish ardor the Americans pursue their own welfare, and to watch the vague dread that constantly torments them lest they should not have chosen the shortest path which may lead to it.
> A native of the United States clings to this world's goods as if he were certain never to die; and he is so hasty in grasping at all within his reach that one would suppose he was constantly afraid of not living long enough to enjoy them. He clutches everything, he holds nothing fast, but soon loosens his grasp to pursue fresh gratifications.... Death at length overtakes him, but it is before he is weary of his bootless chase of that complete felicity which forever escapes him.[20]

Taken together, Tocqueville's discussions of individualism and materialism capture the essence of proprietary equality in America. In so doing he caught the contradiction that is equality in a liberal-capitalist society: people "born equal" hastening to become unequal.

Having dealt with the source and nature of equality in America as well as the characteristics of the process undermining it, Tocqueville examined what he understood as the reason for continuity in American thinking, not merely with regard to equality, but about most political matters. He minced no words. In chapter 15 of his first volume, where he made his well-known argument about the tyranny of the majority, Tocqueville wrote: "I know of no country in which there is so little independence of mind and real freedom of discussion as in America."[21] Of course, Tocqueville persisted in his error of attributing this "despotism" to the existence of equality rather than to the requirements of private capital, but his description of the situation is both accurate and timely:

> Fetters and headsmen were the coarse instruments that tyranny formerly employed.... Such is not the course adopted by tyranny in democratic republics; there the body is left free, and the soul enslaved. The master no longer says: "You shall think as I do or you shall die"; but he says: "You are free to think differently from me and retain your life, your property and all that you possess, but you are henceforth a stranger among your people. You may retain your civil rights, but they will be useless to you, for you will never be chosen by your fellow citizens if you solicit their votes; and they will affect to scorn you if you ask for their esteem. You will remain among me, but you will be deprived of the rights of mankind.[22]

These words, written almost a century and a half ago, continue to sound a clear warning today; a warning especially pertinent in light of the presently rising conservative tide with its accompanying tendency to brand unconventional views heretical and subversive. Tocqueville perceived, with others,[23] that Americans are prone to intolerance toward ideas which are apprehended as running counter to conventional wisdom. As regards our concern here, Tocqueville warns us that alternatives to proprietary equality—that "bootless chase of complete felicity" endemic to liberal-capitalism—confront obstacles ranging from apathy to hostility, both obstacles being a result of the self-evident dominance of possessive individualism. Tocqueville thus instructs us about the roots of our present condition as well as about obstacles in the path of an alternative future.

Despite the continuing accuracy of Tocqueville's insights into the nature of American equality and the uniformity of opinion about it, the conviction prevails in the folklore of this country's politics that, as one analyst put it, there is more than a "dime's worth of difference"[24] separating the two political parties in the United States. Whether the cliche should be modified to reflect the ravages of inflation or not, the point is that, contrary to what many journalists and political scientists often say, our two parties do not disagree over the basic character of liberal-capitalist society. Of course, Democrats and Republican differ in the sense that they offer two variations on liberal capitalism, but neither transcends its confines.

This section is an examination of nineteenth-century American thought and practice with respect to the liberal norm of equality. Its purpose is to revise our mythology about equality by examining continuities among two historical periods generally assumed to represent diametrically opposed tendencies. The first period is that of so-called Jacksonian Democracy extending roughly from 1825 until 1850. The second is the conservative Republicanism which prevailed, once again roughly, from 1870 until the election of Franklin D. Roosevelt in 1932. Stereotypically, these times are conceived as being the age of the People versus the age of the Plutocrat respectively. As with all myths, these contain a kernel of truth. It is certainly true that the ethos of the periods differed. Individualized acquisaition was, shall we say, democratized in the context of the open frontier during the earlier period and rendered an exclusive preserve during the latter one. What this means is that proprietary equality prevailed in both times. What changed was the extent of participation, from the many to the few.

In terms we have used to analyze the roots of proprietary equality, the Jacksonian period might be said to have witnessed a more amiable, Lockean emphasis upon the right of Americans to pursue wealth unfettered by governmental restraints. Following the Civil War, a harsher, we might say Hobbesian, persuasion held sway, emphasizing the internecine struggle for survival of the fittest. The analysis in this section consists of several basic points: (1) although differing in emphasis, both periods illustrate the predominance of proprietary equality in liberal-capitalist America; (2) in neither period did the prevailing emphasis exist to the exclusion of its counterpoint within liberal ideology; (3) never did either faction raise fundamental alternatives to proprietary equality (except, perhaps, as strategic nods in the direction of the fringes of American politics intended solely to co-opt those on the margins of society).

The Jacksonian Persuasion, as historian Marvin Meyers titled his study of the political movement inspired by the president whose name it took, was thoroughly proprietary in its orientation. At its core was an attack, *not* on individualized acquisition, but upon all forms of privilege and encumbrance which served to exclude or inhibit segments of the American public from that very pursuit of private enrichment all assumed to be their birthright. As such, Jacksonian politics was not the alien subversion of all American values and institutions that its detractors made it out to be. Indeed, so far was it from being un-American that the Jacksonian persuasion entrenched, one might say enthroned, proprietary equality, broadening its appeal by generalizing its participation. Jacksonians thus did not challenge the underlying liberal character of equality in the United States; rather they sought to give more people a stake in it. Speaking colloquially, Jacksonians liked the taste of the American pie; they simply objected to the way in which it was sliced.

Professor Meyers aptly characterized them as venturous conservatives. It is significant that Meyers derived this interpretation from Alexis de Tocqueville's reflections. Meyer is convinced, as are we, that Tocqueville had his hand on the pulse of Americans during this period. Of Tocqueville's image of the Jacksonian Democrat, Meyers wrote:

> As Tocqueville abstracted the democratic type from his Jacksonian observations, so I think one can profitably reverse the process, reviewing Jacksonian times in the light of Tocqueville's synthesis. His image of the venturous conservative pervades much of my discussion of the Jacksonian Persuasion. Tocqueville does not himself make the connection between social situation, typical response, and the specific content of the Jacksonian political appeal; yet it seems to me a highly plausible association. The American who was involved in the continuous re-creation of his social world, the continuous relocation of his place within it, became the anxious witness of his own audacity. The consequence, Tocqueville suggests, was the renewal of frenetic activity and, at the same time, a powerful attachment to property and order. A further response is evidenced, I would propose, in the effectiveness of the Jacksonian political appeal: to hard money, personal enterprise and credit, rural simplicity, and broadly, to the pristine values of the Old Republic.[25]

We suggest that these elements comprising the Jacksonian world view imply strongly a notion of equality centered upon the rights of every individual to get (and stay) ahead. Venturous conservatives thus are separated from their political opponents in America by the numbers of people they desire to include in the process of capitalist accumulation. This acquisitive concept of equality occupies a central position in the platforms of so-called American liberals throughout our history. There is a direct lineage running from the Jacksonian "man of enterprise" through the Wilsonian "man on the make" to the present-day "liberal" emphasis on affirmative action in the context of a welfare state. Common to all three is the conviction that equality amounts to the individual right to participate in private accumulation. The crucial point is that this is a peculiarly capitalist definition of equality. Proprietary equality presupposes the capitalist principle that growth per se is not only beneficial, but that it alone serves as the vehicle for expanding equality. Its logic holds: the more capitalist accumulation is encouraged, the larger the aggregate resources, hence the greater number of people that can be included. The "liberal" version of proprietary equality is thus tied to the *expansion* of private appropriation: make every American a capitalist. As we said, American liberals have supported this strategy in the name of egalitarian sentiments from the age of Jackson up until the currently fashionable conservative retrenchment of the late 1970s and early 1980s.

We can observe the Jacksonian incarnation of this position in the writings of prominent spokesmen for the movement. The editorials of William Leggett (1801-39)—author, journalist, and "one of the hardest hitting of the radical Democrats,"[26]— for example, reiterate one of the keynote themes of Jacksonianism: the inclusive rights of property. In an editorial entitled "Objects of the Evening Post," Leggett wrote:

Those who only read the declamations of the opponents of the equal rights of the people may be induced to believe that this paper advocates principles at war with the very existence of social rights and social order. But what have we asked in the name of the people that such an interested clamor should be raised against them and us? What have we done or said that we should be denounced as incendiaries, striking at the very roots of society and tearing down the edifice of property?...Does it savor hostility to the rights of property to maintain that all property has equal rights and that exclusive privileges granted to one class of men or one species of property impair the equal rights of all the others?...In pointing out what we believe errors in former legislation and recommending their abandonment in the future, do we violate any right of property or recommend any breach of public faith? Or, in advocating the equal rights of all, do we impair the constitutional rights of any?[27]

Daniel Henshaw (1791-1852)—author, businessman, and Jacksonian politician— in a commentary on the Dartmouth College case, articulated the Jacksonian corollary to their principle of inclusive property rights, denial of exclusive privilege. *Dartmouth College v. Woodward* (1819) raised issues involving the prerogatives of state legislatures and, most germane to the present discussion, the obligations of contract. The Supreme Court held on behalf of the "old" trustees of Dartmouth, against those appointed under the aegis of legislation passed by a Republican majority in the New Hampshire legislature, thus upholding the original contract.[28] Henshaw, representative of Jacksonians, saw the Marshall Court decision upholding contracts against legislative action as an anathema. He wrote:

If the appointment of men to office be a contract, charters of incorporation contracts, and marriages be a contract, as Judge Marshall pretty plainly, and Judge Story [another member of the *Dartmouth* majority] unequivocally, intimates, coming within the scope of the before-cited inhibitory clause of the Federal Constitution [Article I, section 10], it would seem to follow that every other transaction of civil society may be engulfed in this vortex and whirled under the jurisdiction of the Supreme Court; and that the people of the states, instead of having governments adapted to their wants, liable to be modified, altered, repealed, or totally changed, as was supposed to be their inherited and unalienable right, have, in fact, *myriads of little perpetuities* beyond the control of state and national legislation, and subject only to the will of their directors or of the lord patrons.[29]

If Henshaw's remarks show the Jacksonian desire to abolish *exclusive* rights of property, the fundamentally capitalist quality of the Jacksonian platform is further demonstrated by the comments of lawyer, author, and journalist Theodore Sedgwick, Jr. (1811-59). Summarizing points he had made under the heading "What Is a Monopoly?" Sedgwick noted:

Here, I have set forth the views of those who style themselves anti-monopolists.... It is not difficult to decide with what justice they have been termed agrarians and jacobians [political epithets of the time used to disparage radical opponents]. It is not difficult to say whether those who labor for equality of right are, in truth, working for a community of property. Property, in itself, is respectable, and the energy and industry by which it is acquired worthy of respect. They are the best friends of property and of men of property who would abolish every unequal and unrighteous means of acquiring it. It is those unequal and unrighteous modes of acquiring it which stimulate the jealousy and arouse the indignation of the less fortunate classes.[30]

The guiding spirit and fundamental commitments of the Jacksonian Period are well summarized by the noted American legal scholar J. Willard Hurst. In his *Law and the Conditions of Freedom in the Nineteenth-Century United States,* Hurst writes of the abiding American passion, described previously by Tocqueville, which gave rise to Jacksonianism:

However inadequately they expressed the vision, people in the nineteenth-century United States had already sighted the promise of a steeply rising curve of material productivity as the dynamic of a new kind of society.... All had in common a deep faith in the social benefits to flow from a rapid increase in productivity; all shared an impatience to get on with the job by whatever means seemed functionally adapted to it, including the law.[31]

This determination to clear all obstacles inhibiting the release of energy, as Hurst puts it, and to create new legal and social institutions to facilitate capitalist development certainly had its peculiarly Jacksonian manifestations. The crucial point, however, is the unanimity which wed Jacksonians to their opponents over the issue of "capital mobilization and discipline," once again using Hurst's terms. At base, Whigs and Democrats agreed that private capital should provide the engine of American prosperity. The sole question at issue was whose private capital. Hurst writes:

Thus the grant of corporate status became a notable issue in the years of Jacksonian Democracy. This did, indeed, involve serious issues concerning the power structure of the society; the Jacksonian polemics on this score forecast the issues in the background of the Granger movement and the Sherman Act. But, aside from the sensitive matter of banks, currency, and credit, the demand for freer incorporation, deep down, fitted the dominant temper of the times, *Jacksonian as well as Whig.* Hence the Jacksonians appear increasingly uncomfortable in their opposition.[32]

As this individualized capitalist growth, underwritten by Whigs and Democrats alike, began to give rise to vast concentrations of wealth and power after the Civil War, the prevailing emphasis within liberalism with regard to equality changed from Lockean polemics to Hobbesian apologetics. This is to say, Jacksonian support for the equal rights of property gave way to Republican defense of existing inequalities. In the course of this transition, advocacy of equal rights to a stake in capitalist accumulation was supplanted by the justification of unequal privilege. The new orthodoxy of the "age of excess"[33] parodied that which it replaced. In the face of tremendous disparities dividing Americans into the very rich and the very poor, it was seriously maintained that everyone still had an equal chance to get ahead. With hard work and a bit of luck, it was said, any American could experience the success of the fictional Ragged Dick[34] or the very real Andrew Carnegie. If people failed, they had no one to blame but themselves. Life was a jungle, Hobbes's state of nature, and only the fittest could (and should!) survive.

By the turn of the century, yesterday's ephemeral facts—equality in America— became contemporary fancies: the idea of what had once been a society in which most white males enjoyed relatively equal chances was held up as an existing reality in order to legitimize the vast inequalities that prevailed. The past was used to bulwark the present. Political scientist Robert G. McCloskey provides an excellent analysis of this process at work:

> The nature of the conservative ideology that developed in the latter half of the nineteenth century begins to be clear. It does not take the form of a sharply distinguishable doctrine counterpoised against the progressive democratic tradition, as in the earlier period. No longer is it practical—or necessary—to inveigh against the shibboleths of democracy. It is far more convenient to make use of the reverence attached to democratic symbols, to harness the horsepower of democracy to the conservative cart. Thereafter, conservatism, far from standing in opposition to democracy, takes its place as an integral part of the democratic value system. Conservatism, to paraphrase a well-worn Communist Party slogan, becomes nineteenth-century Americanism.[35]

In this manner did Social Darwinism co-opt the coveted center of American politics. The defining characteristic of this Americanism was, as noted just above, a Hobbesian war of each against all. "Homo homini lupus," wrote Hobbes: each man is a wolf to every other man. This was a theme which ran through the Gilded Age like a scarlet thread. McCloskey writes that the "robust conservative doctrine" was a compound of "Spencerian Darwinism, Malthusianism, and classical economics." Such it was. Still, all three are Hobbesian to their core: the survival of the fittest, the horrors of geometrical population growth checked only by the Four Horsemen of the Apocalypse, and the propensity to compete among humans defined as given solely to trucking and bartering—all bear striking affinity to Hobbes's characterization of human behavior in a state of nature.

In 1651 Hobbes had listed first among his dour catalogue of the qualities of mankind the "love of contention from competition. Competition of riches, honor, command, or other power, inclineth to contention, enmity, and war: because the way of one competitor, to the attaining of his desire, is to kill, subdue, supplant, or repel the other.[36] Jacksonian Democracy's support of equal rights for property— what Tocqueville described as the bootless chase—had resulted in creating and justifying *un*equal rights of property. What counted in the late 1800s was making money. Tocqueville's America had inevitably degenerated into ceaseless grubbing after financial domination. Historian Ray Ginger describes the consequence in this fashion:

> "Get money—honestly if you can, but at any rate get money! This is the lesson that society is daily and hourly dinning into the ears of its members," wrote Henry George in *Progress and Poverty*. Doubtless men tend to think always that an earlier time was a happier time. But the unversality of this apprehension does not prove it is never true. The Mark Twain who wrote *The Adventures of Huckleberry Finn* was certainly aware of the human evil in the United States before the Civil War. But he recalled that nobody in his youth had worshiped money and that none of the well-to-do men of the neighborhood had been accused of getting rich "by shady methods." Twain, along with other observers so diverse that they would have agreed on little else—Henry Adams, Willa Cather, William Dean Howells, Edith Wharton, Walt Whitman— thought that the acqusitive spirit increasingly held dominion. Not only was the desire to make money checked by fewer other values, but men were able to make vastly more money by exploiting new products and new techniques.... Buck Duke [James Buchanan Duke], a great admirer of John D. Rockefeller, analyzed as follows the policies that had guided his hero to virtual monopoly: "First, you hit your enemies in the pocketbook, hit 'em hard. Then you either buy 'em out or take 'em with you."[37]

The substance of this Hobbesian emphasis in liberal-capitalism can be illustrated in the work of several prominent conservatives. A more revealing person to begin with can hardly be found than William Graham Sumner. Sumner, writes McCloskey, "supplied the premises for what came to be known as 'the gospel of wealth'; he was the schoolmaster, the grammarian, of the new conservatism."[38] Sumner's teaching was a pungent amalgam of skepticism, capitalism, and integrity. In the first place, Sumner held a dim view of human nature. Rivaling Hobbes for misanthropy, he ascribed "four great motives common to men—hunger, love, vanity, and fear."[39] Humans were perceived to be unchanging in their self-centered pursuit of gratification, often (with relish) at the expense of others:

Thus the operating virtues approved by the Sumnerian ethic are those that promote material well-being, and from here—given the assumptions of classical economics and Social Darwinism—it is a simple step to say that the good man is he who most single-mindedly seeks to promote his own well-being. Selfishness is raised to the status of an absolute good; the Hobbesian man becomes the moral ideal.[40]

There should be no doubting that Sumner's ideal man was synonymous with capitalist man. Sumner's premises were in tune with the essentials of the rampant laissez faire capitalism permeating his time. The accumulator of capital was the paragon of Sumnerian virtue. It was the entrepreneur—innovative, ruthless, free-wheeling—who provided not only for his own security but for the progress of society as a whole. His ventures must not be obstructed. Much better to let capitalists have their way than to regulate the sole means of generating the preservation of the species. McCloskey characterizes the central features of Sumner's capitalism in this manner:

Fitness, on Sumner's postulates, means of course fitness to contribute to the material welfare of society. "Let it be understood that we cannot go outside of this alternative: liberty, inequality, survival of the fittest; not—liberty, equality, survival of the unfittest. The former carriers society forward and favors all its worst members." It is true that unregulated entrepreneurship will produce millionaires and monopolists. But this is not to be regretted.... Great inequalities of wealth therefore are not only to be tolerated; they are to be encouraged. The free working of the market will produce monopolists. These monopolists will attempt to impose their will on society in the form of plutocracy. But all of these seeming evils must be endured, so that society can enjoy the benefits which the millionaire showers upon it.[41]

The crucial point in this is that Sumner assumed that every human has the equal opportunity to exercise the self-denial required to accumulate capital and become (eventually) a monopolist/benefactor. Sumner believed that one person's gain was not necessarily another's loss: "Thus the struggle is like a whippet race; the fact that one hound chases the mechanical hare of pecuniary success does not prevent the others from doing the same."[42]

Stephen J. Field, associate justice of the Supreme Court from 1863 to 1897, provides a second illustration of the sort of Hobbesian liberalism that prevailed in the United States during the second half of the nineteenth century. In fact, Field's sort of liberalism dominated the Court until Franklin D. Roosevelt's abortive court-packing attempt and the consequent "switch in time that saved nine" in 1937. Field is thus representative of a powerful bloc of jurisprudential opinion: "His thirty-four years on the bench of the Supreme Court...almost exactly correspond with the growing period of the conservative ideology.... Field was to the Court what the great crowd of conservative publicists was to the country at large—a gadfly, an instructor, and a prophet."[43]

Field's impact on American constitutional law corresponds, more or less, with the rise of the doctrine of substantive due process. More precisely, he and his colleagues bent the concept to the purposes of capital. As it was understood during Field's tenure on the Court, substantive due process amounted to the Court's maintaining that it had the prerogative of exercising ultimate judgment with regard to the substance of legislation, particularly economic regulatory legislation. Substantive due process thus established the Court as a supraregulatory body reviewing the police actions of state and federal legislatures. In effect, of course, the doctrine resulted in, as Justice Holmes put it in his famous dissent in *Lochner* v. *New York* (1905), "enact[ing] Mr. Herbert Spencer's *Social Stacs.*" Holmes continued a bit later, "A Constitution is not intended to embody a particular economic theory, whether of paternalism and the organic relation of the citizen to the state or of laissez-faire." Whether or not Holmes's notion about the pristine economic character of constitutions (and te American Constitution in particular) is correct can be debated. Nevertheless, his criticism of his colleagues in the majority on *Lochner* hits the mark: they consistently equated "constitutionality" with the requirements of capital.

Two central, related features of Field's world view were the absolute rights accorded to property and the sanctity of contracts. Field assumed that property was sacred, despite who (or what) owned it, what quantities were owned, or to what purposes it was put. Likewise, parties to a contract were assumed to come to the agreement as equals in need of no protection, and, once bound, as having entered into an inviolate pact; this, once again, despite differences between the strength of parties, circumstances surrounding the arrangement, or the aims being sought. That Field brooked no restrictions upon these rights may be seen in his dissenting opinions written in *The Slaughterhouse Cases* (1873) and *Munn* v. *Illinois* (1877).

In the former opinion Field offered an interpretation of the phrase "privileges and immunities" contained in Article IV, section 2 of the Constitution. Adopting the position of Justice Washington in *Corfield* v. *Coryell* (1823), Field wrote:

Mr. Justice Washington said he had "no hesitation in confining these expressions to those privileges and immunities which were, in their nature, fundamental...." They might be "all comprehended under the following general heads: protection by the government; the enjoyment of life and liberty, with the right to acquire and possess property of every kind, and to pursue and obtain happiness and safety; subject, nevertheless, to such restraints as the government may justly prescribe for the general good of the whole." This appears to me to be a sound construction of the clause in question. The privileges and immunities designated are those which of right belong to the citizens of all free governments. Clearly among these must be placed the right to pursue a lawful employment in a lawful manner, without other restraint than such as equally affects all persons....

In the *Munn* opinion Field elaborated upon his views with specific reference to property and liberty of contract:

All that is beneficial in property arises from its use, and the fruits of that use; and whatever deprives a person of them deprives him of all that is desirable or valuable in the title and possession. If the constitutional guaranty extends no further than to prevent a deprivation of title and possession, and allows a deprivation of use and the fruits of that use, it does not merit the encomiums it has received. ... No state "shall deprive any person of life, liberty or property without due process of law," says the Fourteenth Amendment to the Constitution. ... By the term "liberty," as used in the provision, something more is meant than mere freedom from physical restraint or the bounds of a prison. It means freedom to go where one may choose, and to act in such a manner, not inconsistent with the equal rights of other, as his judgment may dictate for the promotion of his happiness; that is, to pursue such callings and avocations as may be most suitable to develop his capacities, and to give them their highest enjoyment.

It should be noted that in construing the Fourteenth Amendment this way Field saw no difficulty in viewing steel corporations and railroad trusts in the same category of "persons" as immigrant employees or farmers, and in maintaining that the latter were equal with the former before the law.

In less than ten years following the *Munn* decision, Field would see his dissenting views command a majority on the Court. The views articulated here are of importance, then, because of their prophetic quality. Field was the bellwether of a "new constitutionalism"[44] that swept to power between 1887 and 1895. He was not, to be sure, the sole exponent of the Hobbesian impulse within American liberalism during this period. Nevertheless, because of his position on the Court, his long tenure there, and his persistent advocacy he left his mark on American constitutional politics.

As final illustrations of the Hobbesian character of the Gilded Age, we turn to two individuals who lived, and prospered mightily, in the midst of the fray: Daniel Drew (1797-1879) and Andrew Carnegie (1835-1919). The former, less well known, was a financier, transportation magnate, and antagonist of Jay Gould and Cornelius Vanderbilt. Carnegie, of course, was an industrialist with vast holdings in steel. Both were, depending upon your point of view, either heroes of American capitalist development or, quite simply, robber barons. Perhaps the truth is they were both. In any event, their lives provide insight into the extremes and complexities of the ideology under study here. Drew serves to shed light on the extremes of the war of each against all that was industrial capitalism in its heyday. He was a rough-and-tumble, no-holds-barred individual who practiced what Sumner and Field preached—and them some! As Matthew Josephson writes:

Born in 1797, in the village of Carmel, New York, in the rural fastness of Putnam County, he had grown up to be a cattle-drover and lived a life of terrible privation in youth, which may have contributed to his "bearish" view of life. The cattle that he gathered up from farmers to drive to New York, purchased on credit, he often never settled for, according to the natives of Carmel; a practice which was the cause of his removing the base of his operations as far as Ohio. To him is also credited the invention of "watered stock," his cattle being kept thirsty throughout the journey, and only given a drink immediately before arrival at the drover's market uptown.[45]

In Carnegie we have a more complex individual. Somewhat more ambivalent about a life devoted purely to accumulation than Drew, Carnegie competed with the most avaricious and won. Committed to philanthropy in his later life, he nevertheless extracted his wealth in authoritarian, monumentally exploitative ways. Writes McCloskey: "The contrast between this ruthless struggle for gain and a personal philosophy of moral humanitarianism is clear enough. But the immobilization of the latter ideal on occasion when the conflict occurred head-on is illustrated and, to a large degree, epitomized in the story of Homestead."[46] Homestead, of course, was the name of Carnegie's steelworks near Pittsburgh, the site of the bloody strike in 1892 that left forty shot and nine killed on the strikers' side and twenty shot, seven dead among the infamous Pinkertons.

Drew and Carnegie do not represent, as one might assume from Carnegie's moral veneer, polar opposites, the former being totally devoid of conscience, the latter naggingly possessed of one. They are cut from the same cloth. If Drew was more explicitly beyond the pale of legitimacy in his tactics, Carnegie was no less predatory. Both men are examples of how the Hobbesian impulse of liberalism in the United States serves to justify inequality. This is our basic point here: both are "self-made men" anxious to reaffirm the availability of opportunities for all in America in order to legitimate their exploitation. As such, they are forerunners of contemporary neoconservatives who seek to justify privilege in America on the basis of notions of merit and vaunted equality of opportunity.

Daniel Drew was given to using aphorisms in his folksy autobiography. One that appears early on in his book captures the spirit of his views: "If a cat would eat fish she must be willing to wet her feet."[47] Drew's lifelong assumption was that any "cat" could enjoy "fish" in America if only it were courageous, audacious, and crafty enough to "get its feet wet." Another Drew aphorism was "When you owe the hen, you get the eggs also." This expression is found in the chapter titled "Gets Control of the Erie" and precedes a passage rife with Hobbesian sentiment. Drew wrote:

It [the panic of 1857] put old fogyism out of date forevermore. The men who conducted business in the old-fashioned, slow-poke method—the think-of-the-other-fellow method—were swept away by this panic.... A new generation of men came in—a more pushful set. I was one of them. We were men now who went ahead. We did things. We didn't split hairs about trifles. Anyhow, men of thin skin, with a conscience all the time full of prickles, are out of plae in business dickerings. A prickly conscience would be like a white silk apron for a blacksmith. Sometimes you've got to get your hands dirty, but that doesn't mean that the money you make is also dirty. Black hens lay white eggs. Take that blacksmith. During the day he gets all grimed up. Then at night he washes, and now is as clean as anything. And his money is clean, too. What better kind of man is there than a blacksmith? It isn't how you get your money but what you do with it, that counts.[48]

Drew's last sentence might correctly be seen as the defining philosophy of Andrew Carnegie's life. How he made his money—the "period of acquisition," as he euphemistically termed it—was not important; how he used his wealth during the "period of distribution"[49] was what counted in assessing his character. Carnegie's gospel of wealth to the contrary notwithstanding, the Hobbesian sentiments exemplifed by Drew are mirrored in Carnegie's life. A revealing clue to Carnegie's views is provided by his statement in his autobiography, "Few men have wished to know another man more strongly than I to know Herbert Spencer, for seldom has one been more indebted than I to him and to Darwin."[50] From Spencer, Carnegie learned the so-called Darwinian lesson: human progress was tied to the survival of the fittest, which was advanced by individual competition. How comforting it must have been to Carnegie to see his life revealed in the work of this eminent social philosopher—"the sage himself," as Carnegie referred to Spencer.

The extent to which Carnegie absorbed Spencer's lessons is underscored in the following passages from Carnegie's book *Problems of To-day*. Following a list of "exceptionals," men who were "workers with their hands (including Shakespeare, Lincoln, Bessemer, Franklin, Columbus, Bell), Carnegie wrote:

All these began as manual workers. There is not one rich nor titled leader in the whole list. All were compelled to earn their bread. Most of them, however, but not all, in due time abandoned labor of the hands, a salutary development, and one to which every working man should aspire.... The dingy room, the close laboratory, the crowded workshop and the home of honest poverty, contain the exceptionals, capable of carrying forward the mission of the race upon earth, which is in each succeeding generation to make this life a little higher and better.[51]

In a subsequent chapter titled "The Long March Upward," Carnegie proclaimed:

Only through exceptional individuals, the leaders, man has been enabled to ascend. He is imitative and what he sees another do he attempts and generally succeeds in doing. It is the leaders who do the new things that count, and all these have been Individualistic to a degree beyond ordinary men and worked in perfect freedom; each and every one a character unlike anybody else; an original, gifted beyond others of his kind, hence his leadership.... Men are not created alike: on the contrary, there is infinite variety, not only in the powers bestowed but also in their degree, for the fruits of men's lifes depend as much upon the amount of the same powers shared with others as upon different powers inherited.... All this Herbert Spencer has clearly revealed.[52]

It seems plausible to argue that what Carnegie intended here was not merely an exposition of his social theories, but his epitaph as well.

Our journey through the regions of American thought with regard to equality has brought us to the place where some reflections are appropriate. The Hobbesian dimension of liberalism dominated well into the first third of the twentieth century, where it foundered on the shoals of the Great Depression and became the subject of attack by supporters of the New Deal. "Foundered" is certainly too strong a word, though. This darker side of American political ideology has time and again demonstrated remarkable resilience: neoconservatism, Ronald Reagan's presidency, and evangelical politics are merely its most recent manifestations.

Returning explicitly to the major concern of this chapter and, ultimately, of our book, by the end of the 1930s genuine equality in America was practically a dead letter. Another way of putting this is to say that liberal-capitalism firmly held the field with regard to the theory and practice of equality in the United States. To be sure, equality continued as an unfulfilled ideal, as a political demand, and as the object of political rhetoric. Nevertheless, to the extent that proprietary equality—a creature of liberal-capitalism—defined the boundaries of legitimate thought and practical action, equality was frustrated. Proprietary equality's Hobbesian dimension never took equality seriously except in terms of shared acquisitiveness; and Lockean reform movements, which provide a kind of alter ego to the more deeply seated Hobbesian American temperament, can do no more than assuage and mitigate the structural inequalities built-up over generations. In sum, what we have reviewed in the foregoing pages is the ideological genesis of what sociologist Michael Lewis termed *the culture of inequality*. A brief overview of Lewis's penetrating analysis will serve to situate us with respect to where proprietary equality has brought us.

Lewis's argument is cogent: professing equality as a social ideal, American culture has developed justifications for persistent inequalities; justifications rooted in what Lewis terms the individual-as-central sensibility.[53] Americans, unwilling to accept the reality of the ways in which capitalism systematically presents unequal chances to different people, yet tied to equality as a social norm, have created over time cultural beliefs which legitimate inequality by explaining it in strictly individualistic terms. According to the culture of inequality, the latest version of proprietary equality in America, the person, not the system, is at fault for inequality's existence. Lewis writes: "Society is seen as benign, offering up opportunities and waiting to be enriched by those who have the will and the capacity to make productive use of them. This sensibility therefore removes inequality of personal perquisites from the category of social conditions in need of reform."[54]

In further support of the thesis presented in this chapter, Lewis demonstrates that the individual-as-central sensibility, first, is the predominant American ideology as regards equality and, second, that this ideology, in ways strikingly similar to proprietary equality, manifests two dimensions: the "moralistic" and the "deficiency" or "therapeutic."

Lewis's first point about the predominance—hegemony[55]—of the culture of inequality complements our argument that proprietary equality pervasively colors American notions about equality. For example, Lewis writes:

The individual-as-central sensibility sets the limits within which widely accepted interpretations of the relationship between individual destiny and what might be termed the morphology of American society develop and are sustained. The sensibility appears to define the range of "respectable" opinion, the universe of discourse within which legitimate differences may occur about the meaning of inequality in American society. It sets the boundaries for "thinkable" ideas about the mitigation of disadvantage, and consequently for "feasible" or "practical" policies concerning inequality.[56]

Second, in a manner congruent with our analysis of the symbiotic Hobbesian and Lockean dimensions of liberal ideology, Lewis contends that the culture of inequality has both a darker and a less self-righteous form. The former, as noted above, he labels the moralistic manifestation of the culture of inequality, the latter the deficiency or therapeutic explanation of inequality. Moralistic explanations locate the source of American inequality in the personal sloth, viciousness, or greed—in a word, immorality—of the disadvantaged. It holds that people are poor, uneducated, imprisoned, because, as immoral individuals, *they deserve to be*. The deficiency explanation, on the other hand, cites as the cause of inequality the personal values, habits, aspirations—in a word, deficits—of the poor. According to this view, people suffer because *they cannot help it*. The moralistic stance leads to feelings of superiority among the nonpoor which give rise to anger, hostility, and insensitivity. The therapeutic position leads to superiority as well, but this turns to pity, condescension, and paternalism.[57] Lewis describes the relationship between the two views:

Despite the existence and significance of...differences, there is more similarity between the standard liberal and conservative positions on poverty and disadvantage than is commonly recognized. Irrespective of the differences between them, both liberals and conservatives appear to view poverty and disadvantage as a function of qualities characteristic of the disadvantaged poor; the two political positions are both derivatives of the individual-as-central sensibility. For the conservative it is the sensibility in its moralistic form, according to which each individual is responsible for his or her destiny without regard for the impact of structural circumstances, which leads to a jaundiced view of ameliorative programs. For the liberal it is the modified form of the sensibility, with its focus on the individualized misfortunes of incompetence and incapacity, which together with an emphasis on deficiency explanations leads to an espousal of the necessity and efficacy of such programs.[58]

In a sobering, some might say frankly pessimistic, epilogue to his study, Lewis addresses the topic "What Will Probably Happen to Us?" It is his conviction that the culture of inequality will continue to hold sway over most Americans. Thus blinded to the structural causes of inequality in this society and, perhaps the more intractable problem, safe in our taken-for-granted assumption that our present views are correct, Lewis says Americans face an unhappy future. He names his scenario a calculus of estrangement. The calculus unfolds in these terms: so-called liberals will grow initially frustrated and eventually completely disaffected from their (expensive, bureaucratic) attempts to save the poor from their own deficiencies; so-called conservatives, in the meanwhile, will grow more smug in their diagnosis of the immorality of being poor and eventually welcome disaffected liberals to their cause. Consequently, Americans will increasingly find themselves divided into two mutually antagonistic camps: the poor, who demand equality, and the rest, who will not (indeed, given the hold the culture of inequality has on them, *cannot*) provide it. "If such a calculus in fact does unfold," writes Lewis, "the culture of inequality will indeed change, but it will change in a way promising an increasingly troubled existence for most of us."[59]

This is not a pleasant prospect. Nevertheless, there are many indications that Lewis's scenario already has begun to unfold: witness the rise of neoconservatism among former liberals, and the support for Reagan's presidency. If we are going to avoid further victimization of all Americans, resulting from proprietary equality's hold upon us, we must conscientiously pursue the aim of this book: critical examination of the theory and practice of equality in America.

SECTION TWO

Where Are We Now?

3

Affirmative Action:
History of An Attempt to Realize Greater Equality

Mary C. Thornberry

It should be apparent from our analysis in the preceding two chapters that we Americans have subscribed in theory to the liberal ideals of equal justice before the law and equal access to political power. Although it took us two hundred years to accept, much less implement, legal and political equality, we now recognize all adult individuals as "legal persons" having certain rights before the law, and as citizens having the right to vote. While convicted felons and the mentally ill are given few of these rights, they are increasingly protected by procedural guarantees of due process.

With respect to social equality, however, our inquiry into American thought shows that we have seldom gone beyond the notion of proprietary equality—a notion of equality of opportunity in the context of an acquisitive society. Part of American mythology is that the United States has been a land of opportunity to which immigrants could come and make their way unimpeded by the barriers of rigid class and status distinctions. Presumably everyone had a chance to be upwardly mobile in this country; through sheer effort, one could "pull oneself up by the boot straps," capitalize on one's opportunities, and be successful. All that was necessary was that everyone have equal access to employment and education; after that, talent and effort would be decisive.

There were, of course, some disturbing reminders that political and legal equality did not obtain for selected segments of American society. Racial segregation in the U.S. Army until after World War II, in southern school systems, in housing covenants, in poll taxes, and in transportation facilities in southern cities indicated that things were not quite right for at least 10 percent of America's citizenry. The "discovery" of poverty and hunger by presidential candidate John F. Kennedy touring Appalachia during the 1960 West Virginia primary was an additional reminder of the existence of great inequalities in income and status.

The debate about the nature of equality which ensued in the early 1960s was usually cast in terms of access to certain goods and services. The most frequently disputed ideas had to do with access to educational opportunities and through them to jobs. Such a focus was not unusual since jobs are the key to income and status in this society and since there are not enough of them—particularly of well-paying, high-status ones—to go around. Secondarily, the debate focused on access to such essential goods and services as health care and housing.

Several conceptions of equality have recurrently appeared in the continuing debate about it which began in the 1960s. One approach in this debate has been to stress the rights people have to the fruits of whatever talents or resources they possess. Not surprisingly, such a starting point is likely to lead to the conclusion that equality is actually not a problem at all. From this point of view the real issue is preserving one's own advantages—whatever the outcome may be in terms of societal inequality. This is the framework used by philosopher Robert Nozick,[1] and his conclusions emphasize that equitable distribution is not so crucial as maintaining title in private hands. Nozick would have us focus on the way property is acquired and transferred through free exchange in society rather than on any specific results of such rules. Justice, for Nozick, results from all members contributing to the common good as they individually conceive or interpret or understand the phrase "the common good," and getting what other members choose to give.

Another approach has been to emphasize the utility of rewarding people according to what talents they can develop that will be used for the good of society. This view lays great stress on the concept of merit and insists that merit ought to be rewarded. While the notion of results is not ignored entirely here, the important thing is to maximize opportunities for the cream of society to rise to the top. It is assumed that those at the bottom of the pile (1) generally deserve to be there and (2) will be served by those who are among the elite. This argument is advanced by several current commentators, including sociologist Daniel Bell.[2] He clearly sees the importance of access to education as a route toward upward mobility in society and argues that the current passion for equality is at war with the accepted and socially necessary concept of meritocracy.

Significantly, neither of these two approaches makes any radical demands for change. Indeed, the first can easily be construed as an ideological justification for a policy of laissez faire, while the second recommends at most gradual changes in education and employment so as to permit the free, unfettered operation of the principles of equal opportunity and differentiation by merit. Both assume a type of legal equality and reject economic equality as necessary or even desirable. They are somewhat unclear as to social equality, although both Nozick and Bell would seem to have serious reservations about any type of imposed equality there.

There is a third alternative, best represented by those who begin with the call for a just society and the need to derive notions of equality from the larger framework of justice. John Rawls is one such writer, and whatever one may think of his specific conditions for a just or fair society, he does force open a wide number of options.[3] In part he insists that status matters as part of equality and that what we value in society may need to be reconsidered. Perhaps because of the complexity of his argument, it has not left academic circles to reach a more popular audience, but perhaps equally as intimidating are the potential requirements for change his argument entails. In a society which glorifies incrementalism, it should come as no surprise that current debate over equality is phrased more in terms of rights and merit than "justice as fairness" and what changes such justice requires.

Given these various justifications for discounting equality or even rejecting it entirely, plus the fundamental sorts of changes required to realize greater equality, it is not surprising that the current public agenda has not made equality a priority item. Apart from the groups which clearly suffer the extremes of inequality, there is little demand for a major overhaul of the liberal-capitalist system. This chapter will explore some of the history of current thinking about equality as it is reflected in the political arena, and examine what the political responses have been.

During the era preceding the Vietnam War, the American public had a brief but significant flirtation with the potential achievement of equality. Because of the insistence of a few leaders within the black community and struggles waged by the civil rights movement, the general prevalence of inequality represented by what sociologist Gunnar Myrdal called the American dilemma was forced on to the national agenda. Among the most forceful spokespersons, of course, was Martin Luther King, Jr. In 1964, before the Southern Christian Leadership Conference annual convention, he said:

Of what advantage is it to the Negro to establish that he can be served in integrated restaurants or accommodated in integrated hotels, if he is bound to the kind of financial servitude which will not allow him to take a vacation, or even take his wife out to dinner? What will it profit him to be able to send his children to an integrated school if the family income is insufficient to buy them school clothes?[4]

The more sensitive of our leaders, men of social conscience such as Hubert H. Humphrey, who had long been advocates of social reform, found an opportunity to press for genuine improvements in the lot of the poor. They were motivated in part by the notion that a just society required government intervention in the workings of society. Their goal was to help the less fortunate succeed. Their immediate strategy was to ensure an equal right to basic necessities, thereby opening options to participation in the American dream. Ensuring adequate health care and educational programs, it was assumed, for example, would enable the poor to break out of the cycle of poverty and to gain their fair share in the wealth of the country.

In the 1970s, a second current in the political approach to equality became evident. An emphasis on productivity, on private initiative, and on desert replaced the generosity which genuine need had triggered. Getting people off welfare became more popular than welfare had ever been. Instead of Lockean talk of a right to basic necessities, there was Hobbesian talk of an equal chance to prove one's individual superiority. Getting ahead replaced helping along.

Part of this second movement was generated by a shrinking economy, which in turn generated a revitalized concern for individual success. Equality had more inherent appeal when it was relatively easy to assume an equal share of an increasingly large pie. The politics of scarcity changed the task of creating a just society into the question of how to preserve one's standard of living.

During the early part of the 1960s, however, when the achievement of equality fleetingly seemed both necessary and possible, there was great stress on removing artificial barriers to genuine equality of opportunity. Aimed first at minorities and then at women, the purpose was to ensure that no unfair hurdles kept these groups out of the mainstream of economic and civic participation. The Equal Pay Act of 1963, the Civil Rights Act of 1964, and the Voting Rights Act of 1965 were all part of this trend. In addition, the Executive Branch issued orders regarding the conditions under which government contracts would be granted, with provisions for including women and minorities in the work force. It is worth exploring at least one of these policies in depth to see what happened. Since it is the executive orders with their ultimate inclusion of the step of affirmative action that have generated the most controversy, we will trace their development in some detail.

One of the first efforts at overcoming discrimination in employment occurred as a result of wartime emergency when President Roosevelt ordered defense contractors "not to discriminate against any worker because of race, creed, color, or national orgin."[5] Given the severe labor shortage imposed by the wartime situation, such an order could clearly be justified as part of the national interest in keeping production at a maximum. During the years which followed the war, executive mandates against discrimination broadened as every president, including Eisenhower, expanded the scope of government intervention. Nondefense contractors, subcontractors, federally assisted construction contracts, and educational institutions were gradually brought under the federal umbrella. The method was to devise standard requirements which automatically became part of every contract the government signed.

As coverage broadened, the basic theory underwent several distinct, if poorly articulated, shifts. From the concept of wartime emergency the emphasis changed to business efficiency, on the assumption that an economy which excluded large numbers of skilled workers from essential jobs could not perform at maximum efficiency. A second shift occurred as a result of the civil rights movement in the sixties; by the end of that decade even the most enthusiastic observers were speaking far less in terms of efficiency than of justice. While the former was a concept dear to the heart of business, the latter was most definitely not.

Also by the mid-1960s it had become apparent that merely outlawing discrimination was insufficient to create genuine equality of opportunity for blacks and other minorities. More positive efforts were necessary if blacks and other minorities were ever to escape the cycle of poverty, ill health, and social dislocation to which centuries of prejudice and neglect had consigned them. As President Lyndon B. Johnson stated in 1965:

Freedom is not enough. You do not wipe out scars of centuries by saying, "Now you're free to go where you want and do as you desire." You do not take a person who for years has been hobbled by chains and liberate him, bring him up to the starting line of a race, and then say "You're free to compete," and justly believe you have been completely fair. Thus it is not enough to open the gates to opportunity. All of our citizens must have the ability to walk through those gates; and this is the next and the most profound stage of the battle for civil rights.[6]

Out of the need to do something more than merely open the gates came the concept of affirmative action. The term was first employed in 1961 when President Kennedy issued Executive Order 10925. Four years later President Johnson issued Executive Order 11246 requiring affirmative action in the struggle for genuine equality of opportunity for all. With the issuance of these executive orders, federal policy had gone through the following shifts: (1) urging nondiscrimination; (2) requiring posting of notice of company policy; (3) introducing the idea of affirmative action; (4) threatening to withhold federal funds for violation of affirmative action. In 1969 a special division, the Office of Federal Contract Compliance, was created in the Department of Labor and was assigned responsibility for reviewing employers' compliance with the terms stated in the executive orders.

Women did not win protection under these executive orders until 1967.[7] However, once sex was added to race as an illegitimate basis of discrimination, women began to use the executive orders to counter long-standing practices of sex discrimination, especially in universities. At the same time, discrimination against minorities in the construction industry came under attack in the Philadelphia Plan. This plan is worth exploring in some detail for the light it sheds on recurring difficulties with the concept of affirmative action. It illustrates the debate about goals and quotas which was later to become crucial for the whole concept of affirmative action.

Fairly early it was recognized that dealing with job discrimination in the construction industry presented special problems. The most obvious difficulty was that workers were not hired in permanent jobs, but rather were selected to work only for the duration of the project. Most job security came through union membership and through union control of job referrals. When the federal government decided to tackle the problem of poor minority representation in the construction industry, it was inevitable that some changes in union apprenticeship programs would have to occur.

Contrary to popular belief, the Philadelphia Plan did not spring full grown like Athena from the fevered brain of an overworked Washington bureaucrat. Rather, several tentative approaches had been tried; Saint Louis, the San Francisco Bay area, and Cleveland had all used some earlier versions of construction-oriented job programs.[8] One of the complaints that contractors had voiced was that after submitting bids and being awarded contracts, they were then subjected to an additional set of specifications in terms of standards to be met for minority hiring. Their usual procedure was to deal with bids where all specifications were clearly articulated. Therefore the government decided to adopt standards for minority hiring which would automatically become parts of any federally assisted construction project. The standards were to be locally developed, with local contractors and unions having opportunities to present evidence as to projections of possible minority participation levels which could be realistically met.

Philadelphia was the first city where these standards were clearly articulated and specific timetables adopted for the whole construction industry. There is still a great deal of controversy over the realism of the standards. However, the issue as it was debated centered on the propriety of government-imposed quotas. We will return to the quota controversy later, but at this stage it is important to note that some specific numerical guidelines were the very things which the contractors themselves had requested in order that they might be able to bid realistically and fairly on contracts.

One further aspect of the Philadelphia story is worth repeating. As dispute mounted, the comptroller general moved to declare that the plan conflicted with Title VII of the Civil Rights Act and therefore could not legally be enforced. The attorney general, John Mitchell, took just the opposite stance, and the dispute eventually went before both houses of Congress. Each chamber upheld the attorney general's stand, thereby giving legislative approval to the executive position.[9] The courts also gave their stamp of approval to both the Cleveland and the Philadelphia experiments. Thus, the legal issues were fairly clearly debated in several forums and settled unanimously in favor of the plan. Affirmative action, in the construction industry at least, was to be part of national policy.

Part of the public controversy over affirmative action stems from a basic misunderstanding of the concept and the policy as well as its requirements. Affirmative action is *not* the same as quotas, nor does the approach insist that factors of race or sex be the sole or even the determining factors in decision making. Broadly speaking, affirmative action measures include a whole range of special steps designed to overcome the consequences of past and present discrimination. These include compensatory and remedial training, validations of tests and criteria for jobs or university admission, the development by employers of recruiting procedures aimed at women and minorities as well as other qualified applicants, provision of child care centers and remedial programs to remove handicaps in employment, and related measures to help the disadvantaged realize their potential. The affirmative action approach also requires employers to examine their work force for underutilization of women and minorities and, where necessary, to set goals or numerical targets for increasing the representation of qualified persons from groups which are underrepresented, with timetables for achieving these targets. Failure to reach the goals set does not result in a governmental penalty (such as loss of a grant or contract) as long as there are valid reasons for that failure and a good-faith effort has been made by an employer to meet them.

Why should a company undertake a policy of affirmative action? Why should it bear the burden of demonstrating that its recruitment policies do not unwittingly contribute to and perpetuate hidden, subtle patterns of exclusion of women and minorities from the work force?

There are at least two answers to this dilemma. One is that unless a company takes some steps to undo its past image, potential job applicants may well assume that there is no hope of gaining employment in that corporation. The second is that proof that the company has changed its policy must lie in the hiring patterns it can produce under that new policy. Without steps to recruit and promote women and minorities, past practices may continue via inertia.

In order to overcome the effects of past practices which resulted in discrimination, companies must now seek out those who were formerly ignored. This is the idea underlying the program. As the regulations themselves specify:

> It is the consequences of employment practices, not the intent which determines whether discrimination requiring remedial action exists. Any employment practice or policy, however neutral in intent, and however fairly and impartially administered, which has a "disparite effect" on members of a "protected class" or which perpetuates the effect of prior discriminatory practices, constitutes unlawful discrimination.[10]

The courts have reaffirmed this thrust as being compatible with the intent of Congress: "Congress directed the thrust of the Act to the consequences of employment practices, not simply the motivation.[11]

Thus employers bear a distinct responsibility even if they have not been part of a conscious effort at discrimination in the past. Just what does the responsibility entail? Official policy statements, appointment of affirmative action officers, development of new recruitment sources, and training of personnel officers are all part of the program. Perhaps the most complicated requirement is an analysis of the present work force and the determination of underutilization. Surveys of the labor force from which recruitment might possibly take place are necessary to determine availability of workers who might be hired. The underlying idea is that, given an equal chance, women and minorities will eventually show up in the job force in proportion to their number in the population at large. There are several potential difficulties with this theory, the most basic being that the very existence of the labor pool is defined in terms of skills which women and minorities often lack.

Let us examine in more detail just how such a policy might operate. Suppose a company has signed a contract with the government which includes the standard promise not to discriminate against employees. One of the first steps it must take is to post notices that it is an equal opportunity employer. Since one sees few notices that any company will refuse to hire minority workers, such steps may not bring any noticeable results in changing the composition of the work force.

The idea of affirmative action is that the company will analyze its own past practices to see where it might have been slighting certain groups. Recruiting friends and relatives of current employees may have the effect of excluding certain groups without conscious planning to do so. An important step is for the company to conduct an analysis of its work force to see how many women and minorities are employed at every level. Having 30 percent of workers be female is not impressive if they are all employed as clericals. At every level the employer is to check to see what the composition is of the labor pool from which hiring is normally done. Thus, if secretaries are normally hired locally, one should inquire as to how many minority secretaries are available on the local level. If sales people are recruited from among college graduates anywhere in the state, then the statistics for racial and gender-based breakdowns should be calculated on a statewide basis. The results must then be compared against the current work force. Where obvious discrepancies exist, the company should set goals to increase minority participation through such tactics as advertising in specialized journals or recruiting at particular schools.

There is another sense in which the term "affirmative action" has become part of the public policy debate. At times, in response to specific findings of discrimination, a judge has ordered a company to take affirmative steps to overcome its own past of demonstrated illegal intent. Unlike the generalized government contracts, these court orders may involve specific quotas which carry real and immediate penalties for violation.

Thus, for example, in January, 1975, in *Commonwealth of Pennsylvania* v. *Rizzo,* U.S. District Court Judge Louis C. Bechtle issued a final order requiring the Philadelphia fire department to hire one qualified minority applicant for every two qualified whites until a nondiscriminatory hiring test was developed. In this case, the judicial remedy of a court-imposed quota was applied because an employer failed to comply with federal affirmative action guidelines. In cases such as this, quotas are direct compensation for discrimination when, because of employers' noncompliance with federal guidelines, individuals have been injured and have suffered from discriminatory employment policies.

While the adoption of affirmative action as an official government policy is an important milestone in the history of the struggle for genuine equality in America, the reaction against the policy is also noteworthy. Criticism has come from a variety of scattered groups. There are several reasons for the opposition. One, the whole issue of racially conscious criteria, will be discussed in detail in the next chapter. At least two others deserve special mention here.

The intensity of public controversy over affirmative action arises in part because a broad range of activities in American life come under the umbrella of affirmative action. As stated above, the necessity of affirmative action was first described in an executive order which contained provisions for contracts between institutions and the federal government. Since many private firms and corporations do business with the federal government, the use by the government of contract stipulations to enforce nondiscrimination and affirmative action has to be counted as one of the more clever strategies of Great Society policy makers. In the threat of withholding a contract should a particular firm refuse to comply with government regulations, the federal government had an immediate and effective enforcement mechanism for its affirmative action policy.

Since government contracts account for a very large portion of American business activity, the nondiscrimination and affirmative action clauses of Executive Order 11246 could and did apply to many different corporations. The regulations applied to subcontractors as well as to major contractors; moreover, if one division of a corporation were awarded a government contract, the contract provisions applied to all divisions and subdivisions of the corporation. If, for example, the physics department of a large university contracted to do research for the federal government, all facets of university life—student admissions as well as all faculty and staff hiring and promotion procedures—would have to comply with the general conditions of government contracts. In short, linking the policy of affirmative action to the practice of government contracts gave the policy clout and ensured that affirmative action would cover a wide range of employees working for many firms in a variety of industries. Affirmative action thus is controversial partly because it has a potentially direct and tangible impact on the fortunes of so many individuals and institutions.

Secondly, like the minimum wage and the social security payroll tax, affirmative action represents an increase in the cost of doing business. It would be foolish to ignore the increased costs in record keeping, in the details of drawing up sound descriptions of labor pools, or in the costs necessary to retrain personnel managers or to validate tests. Such burdens can lead to increased costs and lowered efficiency in the short term. Part of the difficulty would seem to lie in the fact that American capitalist industry has fragmented itself and been reluctant to share information. Materials on descriptions of local and national job markets and on test validation are obvious candidates for pooled resources.

The most often voiced criticism of the concept of affirmative action, however, is that it inflicts burdens on members of the majority who are excluded from jobs or educational opportunities because of their majority status. Sometimes the issue is phrased as reverse discrimination, although that wording itself suggests that the majority members may have some inherent rights which others vigorously dispute. It is that concept and the celebrated *Bakke* case to which we turn in the next chapter.

4

Problems of Implementing Affirmative Action I: *Bakke* and Equal Educational Opportunity

Mary C. Thornberry

Although few Supreme Court cases have excited public discussion the way the claims of Allan Bakke did, neither the publicity surrounding the case nor the decision of the Court seems to have done much to achieve a consensus on the issues presented. This chapter will review the background of the case, examine some of the ways of presenting the issues, analyze the response of the courts, and explore some of the matters which were left unsettled.

The setting of *Regents of the University of California* v. *Bakke* was a state (California) and an era (early 1970s) in which official discrimination had come to an end. Yet, equality seemed no nearer for many people, and the riots in Watts remained a symbol of frustrations that had no easy solutions. Segregation and poverty continued. One of the many aspects of the general inequality was the lack of access to higher education for almost all minority groups.

Strictly speaking, the *Bakke* case did not involve the issue of affirmative action since the program he challenged was focused on university admissions rather than faculty or staff hiring. Yet, it was linked with the debate on affirmative action and grew out of the same political background. In the late 1960s, many institutions of higher education, including law and medical schools, voluntarily initiated programs designed to alter the extraordinarily low rate of minority participation in higher education. Such programs were undertaken partly in response to the civil rights movement and the urban unrest of the sixties, and partly because of an increasing awareness that equal opportunity in employment seemed impossible to achieve without something approaching equal educational opportunity for minorities and women.[1]

Therefore, when the University of California opened a new medical school at Davis, the faculty quickly decided that some special program was needed to make sure that minority students would make up a significant portion of the future doctors of the state. A separate entrance program was established for disadvantaged applicants, and 16 of 100 places were set aside for applicants from that program. Although the same criteria were used for both the regular and the special admissions program, lower standards were sufficient to gain entrance if one could qualify under the disadvantaged program. Whites were not allowed to apply under that program even if they came from a lower income background. The program was successful in bringing in minorities in increasing numbers. Only 7 blacks and Chicanos came in under the general admissions program from 1970 to 1974, but 59 qualified under the special admissions program. For Asian-Americans the record was more mixed: 41 were admitted under the regular program and only 12 under the special one.

Bakke's objections were that he was precluded from competing for 16 of the 100 slots on the basis of race and that his qualifications were generally superior to those of many of the disadvantaged entrants. The university conceded that it could not prove that Bakke would not have been admitted if the special program had not preempted those slots. Thus the stage was set for what came to be known as the issue of reverse discrimination.

Part of the difficulty which the *Bakke* case presented was the variety of perspectives which existed about the basic issue. There were more than two sides to this story. Three of the perspectives will be examined here: the issue of reverse discrimination, the issue of the relevance of race, and the questions relating to compensatory social policy. The larger questions about the nature of the society in which such choices have to be made will be addressed later in the book.

It should be noted that reverse discrimination is difficult to define with precision and has, in fact, been identified in several different forms in public debate:

(1) as hiring unqualified in preference to qualified candidates because of sex, race, or minority status;

(2) as hiring less qualified over more qualified applicants in situations where all are minimally qualified for a position;[2]

(3) as hiring one of two approximately equally qualified persons because of race or sex (here the factor of sex, race, or minority status is used to break a tie).[3]

Preferring unqualified to qualified candidates because of race or sex is very difficult to defend from a moral point of view; one would have to justify the sacrifice of standards of quality, the resulting failure to respect consumers' rights to the best possible service, and the inconvenience suffered by qualified candidates whose legitimate expectations and aspirations have been disappointed and unfulfilled. Moreover, preferring unqualified to qualified candidates because of race or sex is explicitly forbidden by the affirmative action guidelines issued by the Office of Civil Rights of the Department of Health and Human Services.[4] However, assuming all applicants are minimally qualified for a position, preferring less qualified to more qualified candidates in order to achieve genuine equality of opportunity for blacks and women may well be morally defensible. In the last category, preferring a black or a woman to a white male to break a tie between two equally qualified individuals may, under present circumstances, be morally preferable to tossing a coin.

In the *Bakke* case the use of the phrase "reverse discrimination" implies that relevant qualifications could be known and ranked and that the less qualified were being admitted in preference to the more qualified. That statement of the issue brings us to the second aspect of this controversy—the relevance of race. One essential aspect of Bakke's argument was that race should be irrelevant to any decision as to who is admitted to medical school. There are several ways of approaching that issue. One problem is the constitutional basis of any notion of equality. Linked to that foundation is the matter of practical interpretation of constitutional history. Have we ever been and can we now afford to be colorblind in all our legal guidelines? Finally, there is the issue of statutory intent. Has Congress given any policy directives on these matters? If so, how do they link up with the constitutional requirements?

The text of the original Constitution makes no mention of equality. It was only with the addition of the Fourteenth Amendment in 1868 and its requirement that all states must guarantee to any person within their jurisdictions equal protection of the laws that equality had some constitutional foundation. Although loath to give the concept a broad interpretation at first, the Court has made use of the clause to guarantee rights of minorities in many areas. Does it apply to the rights of majorities as well? While the *Bakke* case was not the first to present this issue, it did force a specific confrontation over the matter of how much protection this clause could afford to those who had suffered no history of slavery or economic oppression. Could there be a double standard for equality?

Lest such an approach sound self-evidently false, let us recall that the Court had already approved a two-tier approach to the equal protection clause: when race is the basis of any legislatively imposed division and where the group has suffered as a result of the standard, the Court has used what it called strict scrutiny, requiring a very high level of justification; when other types of classifications are involved, the Court has been content to rely merely on a standard of legislative reasonableness. Thus one possible approach to the issue of constitutional equality would be to say that strict scrutiny applies to cases where minorities are being deprived but that legislative reasonableness will suffice for instances in which they are being aided.

Linked with the matter of constitutional meaning is the reality of American history and our treatment of minorities. Certainly the Fourteenth Amendment itself was originally designed to help overcome some specific historical mistreatment. The record of enforcement of that provision as well as other constitutional and statutory measures is one of halting incrementalism at best and recurring and demeaning discrimination at worst. Voting participation, housing patterns, medical care, educational opportunities, job distribution, and income and status levels all reflect the persistence of racism in the United States. Can we at this stage call upon all people to be colorblind when we have been so deliberately, hurtfully color-conscious throughout our history? Is it only when advances seem in sight that this tactic, reverse discrimination, is adopted as yet another means of delay?

Another way of presenting the issue of the meaning of the laws is to examine not just constitutional foundations but also the structure which Congress has chosen to build in the way of statutory provisions regarding equality. There are many laws which outlaw discrimination on the basis of race, one of which has some direct bearing on *Bakke*. Title VI of the 1964 Civil Rights Act provided that

"No person in the United States shall, on the ground of race, color, or national origin, be excluded from participation in, be denied the benefits of, or be subjected to discrimination under any program or activity receiving Federal financial assistance."[5]

Did Congress intend to protect the interests of the white majority as well as of the minority members? Certainly the wording of the statute is in racially neutral terms and does not exclude whites. On the other hand, it is true that the possibility of reverse discrimination had not yet appeared on the horizon when the law was passed, and the historical circumstances which led to its adoption were rooted in discrimination by the white majority against the black minority.[6]

Bakke's perspective was that while the laws may have been founded in one historical context, they were written to give protection to all—the white majority included. He and his lawyers argued that to perpetuate racial barriers, even in the cause of improving the lot of the minority, was to perpetuate racism. Who would be entitled to the concept of special protection and for how long? Was it not patronizing to assume that certain races would never compete without the benefit of special advantages? Bakke thus advocated a program of immediate racial neutrality and the abolition of race as a valid criterion for admission to medical school.

The University of California and its allies argued that there were several reasons that race could, and should, be used as a specific part of an admissions program. The first was to help overcome the lack of minority members in the medical profession. Only two black medical schools existed, for example, but they produced about two-thirds of the nation's black doctors. While the total black population neared 11 percent, black physicians were only 2.2 percent of the nation's doctors. Under the regular admission program the same pattern seemed to be repeating itself; only one black qualified under that standard in the years 1970 to 1974. Part of the concern was that bright black youngsters would perceive the health professions as a white enclave and not consider the possiblity of a career in medicine.

Tied to the lack of black physicians was the lack of health care available in many rural and inner-city regions across the country. Some were arguing that it would take minority members to understand the problems of these areas. Others seemed to stress that the underprivileged would simply be more likely to return to disadvantaged areas. In either case, it was felt that recruiting students from these areas would, in the long run, help solve one of the major problems in the health care delivery system of this country.

Another factor which underlay the university's concern for racial standards was a recognition of historic discrimination against these groups, which had encompassed far more than medical school admissions. Segregation which began in early grade school, which was reflected in housing patterns, in income distribution, and in isolation into separate job categories—these were historic facts in which the state of California had participated to some extent. While this admissions program was only a small step, it was seen in part as restitution for past injustices.

While these three factors dealt with social policy and social issues in broad terms, there was also a fourth and narrower justification which the university offered for its special admissions system. It felt that the diversity of the student body was an important part of the educational experience which it was trying to organize. If there were no minority members in the class, other students might fail to realize some of the problems unique to those groups. Perhaps including some of the minority students would make the total group of future doctors more aware of ghetto conditions and more motivated to help solve problems there.

Thus the case came before the Supreme Court representing a number of themes. There was the issue of congressional intent in the passage of Title VI of the 1964 Civil Rights Act and its application to this case. There was the problem of the proper interpretation of the Fourteenth Amendment's equal protection clause, especially as related to the white majority. There were the specific historic injustices which the university claimed to be redressing. Over all there was the emotion-charged cloud of reverse discrimination which had become ominous, threatening to unleash torrents of invective. It seemed that there was no way the Court could avoid causing a public outcry in reaction to its decision, whatever that decision would be.

As it turned out, the Court's decision was something of an anticlimax. Badly divided, the Court produced a four-one-four decision, with Justice Powell trying to build a narrow bridge between two sharply split camps. Perhaps the position easiest to understand is that signed by Justices Stevens, Burger, Stewart, and Rehnquist, who approached the issue from the standpoint of Title VI. They urged the Court to abide by the rule that constitutional issues should be avoided wherever possible, especially if mere statutory interpretation suffices to deal with a case. In this instance, they argued, Title VI clearly allowed no consideration for racial characteristics in determining who could benefit from federally funded programs. Since the medical school at Davis received federal funding, they felt that Title VI blocked the use of race as a criterion in the admission process.

The opposing group of four justices, composed of Brennan, White, Marshall, and Blackmun, all wrote separate opinions which tended to stress slightly different points. They were united, however, in believing that race was a valid criterion when it is intended to help and not to hurt groups which have suffered in the past. Not only did they read Title VI as not applying to a *Bakke*-type situation, they also rejected its applicability because they felt that it did not grant a private right of action. That is, they argued that only the attorney general had the privilege of bringing suit under its provisions, while an individual such as Bakke could not. Relying heavily on the congressional debate which preceded adoption of the 1964 Civil Rights Act, they quoted many sponsors of the law to illustrate that its clear intent was to prevent discrimination against minority groups. In turning to the Fourteenth Amendment, they read its provision in the context of protecting the weak against the strong. While acknowledging the need to look carefully at any use of race to make sure that some subtle new form of harassment had not been devised, they allowed racial classifications to stand if convincing reasons were given. To these four justices the University of California in its list of reasons had established sufficient cause to permit the use of race in a medical school admissions program. Justice Marshall included an impassioned review of the treatment of blacks in this country to undergird this need for more than neutrality. Justice Blackmun argued that the need for incorporating minorities made the use of special programs necessary in order to fulfill the demands of equality.

It is Justice Powell's opinion which has attracted the most attention because it provided the necessary yet fragile link between these two camps. Powell was willing to assume a private right of action under Title VI, but he asserted that the ultimate interpretation of Title VI should be linked to interpretation of the Fourteenth Amendment. His interpretation of these crucial documents was that all Americans are to be treated identically: minorities should not be given special considerations that others do not enjoy. Thus he rejected the Brennan camp's contention that either Title VI or the Fourteenth Amendment is restricted to "discrete and insular minorities." Equal protection was a right of all persons and not only of some specially designated inferior groups. In the absence of a finding of specific discrimination traceable to a particular institution, there should be no explicit use of race as a general criterion for any remedial benefits.

Such reasoning undercut the three general rationalizations which California had offered for its program. Since the medical school itself had not been responsible for past discriminatory treatment, it could not start a system of its own to remedy such treatment if the remedy involved racial standards. As to the need to get more physicians into the underserved areas, Powell felt that there were "more precise and reliable ways" of accomplishing that objective. Any efforts to build in explicit racial quotas were rejected by Powell as "facially invalid."

There was, however, a legitimate concern for a diverse student body, a concern which could be met by using race as one of several criteria. In citing approvingly the admissions plan which Harvard University had adopted, Justice Powell noted that there were no fixed quotas and hence no slots for which whites could not compete. Instead of a system of set-aside seats, a system of bonus points allowed disadvantaged blacks to compete more equally for each seat. Such a plan, although not blind to racial criteria, did not use race to guarantee fixed results. Such a system, Powell felt, was consistent with the Fourteenth Amendment guarantee of equal protection.

It is significant to note that the justification for the Harvard Plan is basically a matter of institutional expediency: instead of being a matter of justice or equality to minorities, the approach is based on what will be of use to the educational institution. As such, it leaves the matter open for the institutional leadership to decide what *its own* needs and priorities are along the lines of admissions policy. Such special programs are hence optional and subject to modification or abandonment.

While the results attending immediately on this case were that Allan Bakke was admitted to medical school and the University of California had to modify its admissions program, there were (and are) several larger issues left untouched. One basic problem is whether the Court itself will ever be able to agree on a framework for addressing such problems pertaining to equality. Sooner or later all the justices will have to decide what the equal protection clause means, especially for the white majority. We shall see in the following chapter how the Court dealt with these issues in the *Weber* case.

Although the Supreme Court has had several occasions over the years to decide cases where the underlying issue involved separation on the basis of race, it has yet to articulate a clear statement of what equality means in a racially diverse society. In the beginning the Court expressed itself in what today would quickly be recognized as the worst kind of racist sentiments. By allowing white supremacy to be upheld as part of the constitutional framework because it happened to be part of the world view supposedly entertained by the framers, the Court put its stamp of approval on oppression of blacks. After the passage of the Fourteenth Amendment, which defined citizenship and established a constitutional foundation for equality, the Court still refused to take seriously the issue of equal treatment for minorities. It first established the notion of "state action" to protect all types of private discrimination and then countenanced state policy under the fiction of separate but equal.[7] Although it gradually tightened its standards for what could qualify as an equal education, the Court nevertheless sanctioned policies which caused generations of minority children to grow up without any hope of genuine equality. Furthermore, in *Korematsu* v. *United States,* the Court gave explicit approval to the worst sort of discrimination, declaring constitutional the "evacuation" of the Japanese community during World War II.

Finally, in the 1954 *Brown* decision, the Court took a firm stand against de jure segregation in the educational field by stating that separation was inherently unequal. Since that time, it has further insisted that positive steps must be taken to overcome past injustices even if such action requires racially conscious measures such as school busing. More recently, the Court has insisted in *McDonald* v. *Santa Fe Transportation Company* that the white race has certain protections under the equal protection clause.

All these decisions only skirt the edge of the problem: deciding just what equality means and how it can be implemented. By now the Court seems to be fairly clear that race cannot be used as a vehicle for legal oppression. It will give careful scrutiny to all classifications based on race to prevent such action. What is less clear, although the *Weber* and *Fullilove* cases discussed in the next chapter speak to it, is how far the Court will go to guarantee equality of results as opposed to mere equality of standards. There is an indication that many of the justices do not agree with Justice Blackmun's statement, "To treat some persons equally, we must treat them differently."

Up to this point, the majority on the Court has not been willing to press for any notion of equality which would encompass assurances of equal position. In several cases, most notably *Griggs* v. *Duke Power Company,* the Court has paid close attention to the differential impact a particular policy has had on one race or another even when such policies seemed to have no obvious racial connotation. At other times, as in *Washington* v. *Davis* and *Milliken* v. *Bradley,* the justices have rejected the notion that achievement of an equal position is necessary to satisfy legal standards of equality. Even though minorities bear unequal burdens because of some public policy decisions, there may be no legal remedy.

Not only has the Court never really resolved what it means to be equal in

America, it also has foreclosed part of that discussion by limiting itself strictly to questions of procedures. To be sure, there are some policies the Court has proscribed—slavery, de jure segregation in public schools, exclusion from voting and jury service on the basis of race. Nevertheless, there is meager indication from the Court as to what equality should encompass in America beyond the fair (i.e., racially neutral) enforcement of whatever standards the white majority happens to adopt. The Court's record on equality, one might say, is very little, very late.

Such a narrow, reluctant attitude caused the Court to ignore many of the hidden questions that the *Bakke* case asks about our society. What does it mean to be a doctor in America? One wonders if the issue would have been as bitterly contested if being a doctor did not imply high status and a right to make a very generous annual income. Not only income and status but power accrues in generous amounts to the leaders of the medical profession. Why are status and wealth so unevenly distributed in the United States? Why is health care so maldistributed? What other options are there for health care delivery?

Another series of neglected questions relate to the concept of merit. The Supreme Court of California, which forbade any consideration of race in admissions, dwelt at length on the idea that Bakke's qualifications were superior to those of applicants admitted under the program for the disadvantaged. Yet, consider the issue of qualifications: What qualities make good doctors? Who is to decide upon those qualities? Must we rely on those qualities which can be most easily measured? Do we want to encourage in-depth psychological screening for potential physicians? Are minority communities best served by white doctors, even highly "qualified" ones? Matters of status equality quickly become linked with notions of legal and economic equality here.

Such questions are undoubtedly difficult and highly topical. One can understand the Court's reluctance to address them. Many of them fall in the category of political questions which probably should engage the Court only in times of emergency. Some simply are beyond the Court's purview. Nevertheless, they are all part and parcel of the narrower issues with which the Court is dealing. We must proceed a bit further in this examination of the limits of traditional approaches to equality in America before we suggest a path to a new theory and practice.

5

Problems of Implementing Affirmative Action II: *Weber* and Equal Employment Opportunity

Mary C. Segers

The *Bakke* case concerned equal educational opportunity and the affirmative measures which universities and professional schools have undertaken in order to broaden educational opportunities for minorities and women. Equal access to education, however, is simply a prelude to equal access to the workplace. It is in the area of equal employment opportunity that the concept of affirmative action is directly pertinent.

In employment, strides have been made on the basis of statutory rather than constitutional law. Title VII of the 1964 Civil Rights Act provided the legal standard of equality in most cases. That act mandated the establishment of the Equal Employment Opportunity Commission to enforce Title VII, which forbade job discrimination. As we have seen, it was the desire to give teeth to the Civil Rights Act which led President Lyndon Johnson to issue the executive orders requiring affirmative action of all federal contractors. Affirmative action, properly speaking, is thus the result of activity by the legislative and executive branches of government, not the courts. The one exception to this rule, we noted above, is mandatory quotas imposed by courts as judicial remedies in cases of proven discrimination.

Like most issues in American politics, affirmative action, despite its origins, ended up being subject to judicial action. In *United Steelworkers of America* v. *Weber* (1979) and *Fullilove* v. *Klutznick* (1980), the Supreme Court handed down decisions more supportive of affirmative action than its ruling in *Bakke.* In this chapter we shall examine the statutes and executive orders upon which affirmative action in employment was based, the Court's ruling in *Weber* and *Fullilove,* and the general problem of reverse discrimination which these cases were said to exemplify.

A new federal policy of equal opportunity in employment emerged by accident as well as by design in the 1960s. The "accidental" plan was the Equal Pay Act of 1963—accidental because the act came about more out of concern for men's pay than for women's.[1] Although first proposed in 1868, equal pay had not really become an issue until women were encouraged to move into men's jobs during the emergency labor shortages of World War I and World War II. In these conditions and throughout much of the early agitation for equal pay, the chief concern of Congress and supporting labor unions was the prevention of women's wages from undercutting men's in jobs traditionally held by males.

Phrased in terms of equal pay for equal work, the Equal Pay Act was an amendment to the Fair Labor Standards Act of 1938 and provided protection only to women who had already been hired to do a job comparable to those being performed by men. Then as now, equal pay was irrelevant without equal access to jobs. There were significant gaps in coverage in the 1963 legislation, and much litigation was required to determine what constituted equal work. One standard evasionary tactic used by employers was to alter job descriptions, adding one extra duty to men's jobs to justify salary differentials.

In 1972, with passage of the Education Amendments Act, the scope of the Equal Pay Act was broadened to include administrative, executive, and professional workers as well as wage and salary earners. Nevertheless, while the *concept* of equal pay for equal work is now generally accepted, the median income for women remains approximately 40 percent below the median income of men. Moreover, it seems clear that equal pay is irrelevant if one cannot get a job in the first place, a problem still confronting women seeking employment (not to mention, in these recessionary times, men also).

Opening up men's jobs to women was a subordinate goal of Title VII of the 1964 Civil Rights Act. Many parts of this landmark piece of legislation were directed at undoing past racial discrimination which had been enforced by state and local governments. The act sought to prevent racial discrimination in public accommodations, public education, federally assisted programs and employment. Title VII was among the most controversial and strongly opposed provisions in the bill. The House of Representatives debated 47 proposed amendments to this provision, while the Senate considered over 500 amendments in three months of floor debate. At the last moment Title VII was amended to include sex as a prohibited category, a move designed more to kill the entire provision than to benefit women.[2]

While the purpose of Title VII was to provide equal job opportunity, the stated means of carrying out this intention involved little more than a prohibition against discrimination in employment. The original law relied solely upon the individual initiative of the victim of discrimination, requiring him or her to file a complaint, and upon the goodwill of the discriminatory employer to end the illegal practices. Title VII did establish the Equal Employment Opportunity Commission (EEOC) as the regulatory agency to implement the law, but EEOC's methods of enforcement were initially weak; its weapons against employers were methods of informal conference, conciliation, and persuasion. Additionally, EEOC was weakened by a kind of divide-and-conquer approach to the job discrimination suffered by women and minorities; it gave top priority to job discrimination abatement concerning blacks and Hispanic-Americans and relatively little attention to sex discrimination as a legitimate area of concern.[3] The

EEOC was also hampered by administrative problems; limited by budgetary restrictions, it began almost immediately to build up a huge backlog of individual complaints—a problem which has plagued it throughout its history.[4]

The Equal Employment Opportunity Act of 1972 expanded both the jurisdiction and powers of EEOC to include three groups of employers previously exempt: educational institutions (public and private), state and local governments, and employers and unions with fifteen or more members (twenty-five was the previous limit). The EEOC was given the right to bring civil suit in all cases except those against government agencies if thirty days of conciliatory efforts were unsuccessful.

In addition to the antidiscrimination requirements of Title VII, most major employers in the United States are faced with the requirements of Executive Order 11246, issued by President Johnson in 1965 and administered through the Office of Federal Contract Compliance.[5] Although the legal requirements of affirmative action may be traced back to Title VII, it derives more specifically from this executive order, which includes requirements such as public advertising of jobs and hiring policies, open and wide recruitment of all candidates, establishing and making available detailed objective criteria for hiring, remedial programs, and child care programs. In addition, the executive order included the setting of goals and timetables for the employment of minority group members in job categories where they are now underutilized.

Initially there appeared to be inconsistencies between Title VII and the executive order, principally with respect to the affirmative actions suggested by each measure. As Schuwerk indicates, these early inconsistencies really involved the doctrine of separation of powers and the notion of checks and balances.[6] Title VII was of congressional origin; the executive order was issued by the president. Title VII permits the courts to remedy the effects of past job discrimination through affirmative action. By contrast, Executive Order 11246 requires federal contractors (holding contracts of $10,000 or more) to voluntarily undertake affirmative action programs whether or not a particular employer has a record of prior discrimination. While Title VII's judicial remedies included a variety of affirmative action measures, it also forbade preferential treatment on the basis of race, sex, color, religion, or national origin. The afirmative action required under the executive order, on the other hand, included analyzing the composition of a company's work force and establishing goals and timetables—frequently misinterpreted as quotas—for increasing the numbers of minorities and women on the payroll.

These apparent inconsistencies did not surface until 1969, when the Department of Labor authorized the Philadelphia Plan.[7] Because Title VII seemed to require less affirmative action than the executive order, some construction firms and labor unions charged that the executive branch of the federal government was exceeding what Congress had authorized. According to Schuwerk, this inconsistency between the two laws was rectified in 1972 when Congress carefully scrutinized the entire program of the executive order as part of its amending of Title VII.[8] Passage of the Equal Employment Opportunity Act of 1972 (which amended Title

VII) thus may be interpreted as congressional approval of the affirmative action requirements of both Title VII and Executive Order 11246. This development became exceedingly important later in the context of lawsuits such as *Weber,* which raised the question whether voluntary affirmative action programs involving preferential treatment violate Title VII of the 1964 Civil Rights Act. The most controversial aspect of affirmative action thus remains the development of goals and timetables and the distinction between goals from quotas.[9]

As we learned from our discussion of the *Bakke* case, at least four justices of the Supreme Court held that preferential treatment in university admissions was inconsistent with and in violation of Title VI of the 1964 Civil Rights Act, which forbids discrimination in federally assisted programs. The *Weber* case posed analogous issues with respect to Title VII: whether a voluntary affirmative action program openly favoring black applicants is outlawed by Title VII, which specifically prohibits racial discrimination in employment. It is to this and other cases of alleged reverse discrimination in employment that we now turn.

As noted earlier in the book, reverse discrimination is difficult to define and has in fact been identified in several different ways in public discussion: (1) as hiring unqualified in preference to qualified candidates because of sex, race, or other minority status; (2) as hiring less qualified over more qualified applicants in situations where all are minimally qualified for a position; and (3) as hiring one of two approximately equally qualified persons because of race or sex ("tie-breaking").[10]

In the continuing debate about affirmative action, all types of reverse discrimination are said to be occurring frequently in the job market. Newspaper headlines and articles in journals of opinion suggest that quality is being sacrificed and standards are lowered as business corporations and institutions of higher education implement affirmative action plans.[11] In scholarly journals, philosophers write lengthy articles justifying or criticizing reverse discrimination without stopping to question whether such discrimination in fact is taking place and without adducing empirical evidence as to its occurrence.[12]

It is, of course, difficult to find evidence of reverse discrimination in its various forms; given the various government statements prohibiting such action and given the risk of lawsuits by aggrieved white males, search committees and personnel departments are not likely to admit that they have flouted existing governmental regulations. No systematic research and very few empirical studies exist on the extent of reverse discrimination. Consequently, the presence and magnitude of the practice remains open largely to speculation. One way of distinguishing fact from rumor would be to examine cases which have appeared in the courts—on the assumption that lawsuits actually filed must reflect fairly solid evidence of reverse discrimination, since it would be futile as well as costly to file suit without reasonable supporting evidence.

In the period 1969 to 1974 complaints filed with the Equal Employment Opportunity Commission by white males amounted to approximately one percent of the total complaints over that five-year period.[13] With respect to university admissions, *DeFunis* v. *Odegaard, Alevy* v. *Downstate Medical Center,* and

Regents of the University of California v. *Allan Bakke* all involved charges of reverse discrimination. One can assume that, while the special admissions program of the medical school of the University of California at Davis was in effect, there may have been other white males whose situation was similar to Allan Bakke's.

In employment, a number of cases have found their way into the courts. *Cramer* v. *Virginia Commonwealth University* involved a white male sociologist's claim that his application for a position in the Department of Sociology was passed over in favor of two women who had lower qualifications and less experience. In *McAleer* v. *American Telephone and Telegraph Company,* Daniel McAleer, a telephone company employee, was passed over for promotion even though he had a higher rating than the woman given the job; McAleer sued and was awarded compensatory damages.

With respect to academic employment, the Women's Equity Action League (WEAL), an offshoot of the National Organization for Women, filed with the OFCC in 1970 a class action complaint of sex discrimination against the University of Chicago, Columbia University, the University of Wisconsin, the University of Minnesota, and the entire state university and college systems of California, Florida, and New Jersey.[14] Charging an industrywide pattern of discrimination, WEAL requested a compliance review of all institutions holding federal contracts (over 90 percent of universities and colleges hold at least one federal contract). As an articulate academic community became aware in this somewhat dramatic fashion of its affirmative action obligations, charges of reverse discrimination multiplied.

Apart from these legal cases, is there other evidence of reverse discrimination to which we can point? One of the few empirical efforts to discover the extent of reverse discrimination was recounted by Barbara Lorch in her "Reverse Discrimination in Hiring in Sociology Departments: A Preliminary Report."[15] In 1972 Lorch sent an anonymous questionnaire to sociology department chairpersons located at 200 four-year colleges and universities in the United States. One hundred and sixty-two (81 percent) of the department chairpersons returned them (a high rate of return which, Lorch noted, indicated strong interest in the topic). Asked whether their institutions had an affirmative action plan, 84 percent of the respondents said "yes," 6 percent said "no," and 10 percent replied they "didn't know."

Of the 162 respondents, 139 stated that their departments had been in a position to hire faculty members within the last two years. Of these, 44 respondents (32 percent) reported that they felt coerced to hire a women or a minority member regardless of whether he or she was the best candidate for the job. The source of coercion or pressure usually was reported as the university or college administration and sometimes departmental colleagues.

The 139 respondents who were in a position to hire faculty were presented with the further question, "Has your department in the past two years bypassed the best candidate for a position in order to hire a woman or a minority member?" Of these respondents, 22 (or 16 percent) marked "yes," 115 (or 83 percent) marked "no," and two reported "don't know." While 32 percent of the department chairpersons *felt coerced* to hire a woman or a minority candidate regardless of whether he or she was the best qualified, only 16 percent *did in fact* practice reverse discrimination. [16] Nevertheless, Lorch maintains that this 16 percent figure indicates a "surprisingly" high degree of reverse discrimination, and she concludes:

The intended or unintended consequence of the HEW guidelines (in addition to employing more women and minorities than previously, many of whom are highly qualified) has been in some cases to *coerce* the administration of academic institutions (in fear of losing federal funds) to in turn coerce academic departments to give preference in their hiring to women and minorities. The result in some cases has been reverse discrimination. [17]

Careful reading of Lorch's article reveals that it is flawed in several respects. While reverse discrimination is never defined explicitly, it is defined implicitly as any hiring policy or decision which takes race or sex into account in any way. Lorch seems unaware of the distinction between "weak" and "strong" types of reverse discrimination. Her espousal of a colorblind, sex-neutral standard—while perhaps commendable in an abstract world of ideal behavior—indicates, especially in light of the refinements others have suggested, an unsubtle, unsophisticated approach to the whole matter. Even a badly splintered Supreme Court in *Bakke* held that race could be one among many factors taken into account. [18]

Secondly, Lorch misunderstands affirmative action. She tends to equate it with preferential hiring and ignores all other aspects of the program. Thirdly, in an effort to show the contradictions of policy regarding affirmative action, Lorch quotes selectively Title VII and HEW guidelines, thereby misrepresenting the government's policy. Fourth, Lorch equates goals with quotas and indicates no awareness of the debate in the literature concerning this important distinction.

While Lorch's figure for actual cases of reverse discrimination (16 percent) seems low compared with informal estimates one hears in conversations with college and university faculty members, it is nevertheless sufficiently high to warrant concern as to how such discrimination may be justified. At the same time, Lorch's failure to distinguish weak from strong reverse discrimination leaves us at a disadvantage, for we do not know how serious these alleged departures from norms of fairness in hiring actually are. By assuming an inflexible and perhaps unrealistic standard of colorblindness and sex-neutrality in hiring, Lorch is able to imply that, in the period she studied, one out of every six white male sociologists was deprived unfairly of a faculty position.

We shall examine the *morality* of reverse discrimination in the next chapter. The *legality* of reverse discrimination in employment depends on a number of factors—for example, whether a program of preferential hiring is court-imposed as a remedy for past discrimination, or whether it is part of an affirmative action plan voluntarily undertaken by an employer to remedy racial imbalances in the work force. The legality of the latter was uncertain until the Supreme Court handed down its decision in June, 1979, in *United Steelworkers of America* v. *Weber*.

The affirmative action plan challenged in the *Weber* case was part of a nationwide agreement reached in 1974 through collective bargaining between the Kaiser Aluminum Chemical Corporation and the United Steelworkers. The agreement covered fifteen Kaiser plants around the country and was designed to remedy the almost complete absence of black workers from skilled jobs in the aluminum industry. At Kaiser's plant in Gramercy, Louisiana, where Brian Weber worked, the area's work force was 39 percent black. But blacks made up less than 2 percent—5 out of 273—of the skilled workers at the plant.

To rectify this kind of racial imbalance, the agreement between Kaiser and the union called for the creation of special training programs open to blacks and whites on a fifty-fifty basis. These special programs were to remain in operation until the number of blacks in skilled jobs reached the proportion of blacks in the labor force from which the individual plants recruited. This goal was to be achieved through parity of promotion; Kaiser would promote one black for one white to new skilled craft positions until blacks constituted 39 percent of the skilled labor force at the Gramercy plant.

To achieve this parity, separate seniority lists of black and white employees were drawn up. Brian F. Weber, a white man who did not have sufficient seniority on the white list but had more seniority than two blacks who had been promoted, sued and argued that the dual list violated several provisions of Title VII forbidding discrimination in employment. Weber's suit was a class action instituted in the Federal District Court for the Eastern District of Louisiana.

The district court held that the training program was unlawful under Title VII because the black workers whom it benefited had not themselves been the victims of illegal discrimination by Kaiser. On appeal, the U.S. Court of Appeals for the Fifth Circuit upheld the lower court. In a two-to-one opinion the appeals court held that Title VII made affirmative action programs permissible only to remedy discrimination against individual employees, not as a response to a perception of general societal discrimination.

The opinion of the appeals court was viewed by the federal government and the civil rights movement as a serious threat to all voluntary affirmative action programs. In order to satisfy the Fifth Circuit Court's requirement that an affirmative action plan be a remedy for past discrimination, an employer would have to admit that it had discriminated and thereby invite Title VII lawsuits from blacks. On the other hand, failure to admit past discrimination would invite reverse discrimination suits from whites such as Brian Weber. Given such a dilemma, employers could be expected to abandon the effort and wait for the government to sue them. The government for its part was also placed in a virtually impossible situation by these lower court rulings. If government agencies had to go out and prove every case of discrimination before an affirmative action program was justifiable, the whole process of integrating the work force could slow to a crawl.

The Supreme Court agreed to review the case in December, 1978, and heard oral argument in March, 1979. On June 27, 1979, the Court, in a five-to-two decision, reversed the lower court rulings and found that private employers such as Kaiser can legally give special preferences to black workers "in order to eliminate manifest racial imbalances in traditionally segregated job categories."[19]

In view of the ambiguity of the Court's ruling in the *Bakke* case—an ambiguity attested to by the fact that both sides in Weber appealed to *Bakke* as precedent to support their argument—the *Weber* decision came as something of a surprise. Whereas *Bakke* had involved constitutional as well as statutory law, the decision in *Weber* turned wholly on statutory construction. At issue was the Court's interpretation of what Congress had done when it passed Title VII of the 1964 Civil Rights Act.

When faced with a question of statutory construction, the Supreme Court routinely and typically examines such matters as the language of the law, the historical context in which the law was enacted, its legislative history (for example, the debates in Congress preceding passage), and the legislative intent of the law's framers and those legislators who voted for it. Justice Brennan's majority opinion in *Weber* was premised largely upon his sophisticated reading of Title VII and is a good example of a broad constructionist approach to statutory interpretation. Justice Rehnquist's strong dissent, by contrast, emphasized a literal, narrow construction of Title VII.

It is clear from Brennan's majority opinion that the Court viewed the Kaiser-United Steelworkers affirmative action plan as a voluntary agreement between private parties whose behavior is not regulated by the Constitution. No question of constitutional law was involved. The justices addressed only the question of whether Congress meant to bar this kind of voluntary action when it outlawed discrimination in employment on the basis of race. As Brennan wrote:

We emphasize at the outset the narrowness of our inquiry. . . . Since the Kaiser-USWA plan was adopted voluntarily, we are not concerned with what Title VII requires or with what a court might order to remedy a past proven violation of the Act. The only question before us is the narrow statutory issue of whether Title VII *forbids* private employers and unions from voluntarily agreeing upon bona fide affirmative action plans that accord racial preferences in the manner and for the purpose provided in the Kaiser-USWA plan.

Justice Brennan conceded that the literal language of Title VII would seem to outlaw racial preference as well as racial discrimination in hiring. That argument, he said, "is not without force." But such a literal interpretation, he continued, "is misplaced," and ignores both the historical context in which Congress enacted the law and the intention of the legislators who voted for it: to improve the conditions of blacks in America. An interpretation of Title VII that "forbade all race-conscious affirmative action," Brennan wrote, "would bring about an end completely at variance with the purpose of the statute and must be rejected." After careful, detailed examination of the legislative debates concerning the Civil Rights Act, Justice Brennan concluded:

It would be ironic indeed if a law triggered by a Nation's concern over centuries of racial injustice and intended to improve the lot of those who "had been excluded from the American dream for so long" constituted the first legislative prohibition of all voluntary, private, race-conscious efforts to abolish traditional patterns of racial segregation and hierarchy.

In his long, biting dissent, Justice Rehnquist argued that "Kaiser's racially discriminatory admission quota is flatly prohibited by the plain language of Title VII." He quoted at length from the floor debates, committee reports, and other legislative history of Title VII to show that "Congress meant to outlaw *all* racial discrimination, recognizing that no discrimination based on race is benign, that no action disadvantaging a person because of his color is affirmative." Rehnquist expressed concern that the majority opinion in *Weber* "introduced into Title VII a tolerance for the very evil that the law was intended to eradicate, without offering even a clue as to what the limits on that tolerance may be.[11]

What made Justice Brennan's statutory interpretation more persuasive than Justice Rehnquist's to other members of the Court? And why was Kaiser's affirmative action plan in this case more acceptable to the Court than the admissions plan of the University of California at Davis in the *Bakke* case? The answers to these important questions have to do with the flexible, nonpunitive, and temporary character of the Kaiser affirmative action plan.

The Kaiser program was temporary, since the promotion plan was to terminate when the proportion of blacks in skilled occupations reached their proportion in the local population. Moreover, while the plan involved a racial preference, it did not involve complete exclusion of whites from the training program and it did not deprive whites of existing jobs in order to give them to blacks. Rather, Kaiser's affirmative action program involved training blacks and whites on a fifty-fifty basis for new openings among the skilled crafts.

Finally, the Kaiser-United Steelworkers plan involved the efforts of institutions in the private sector, not public agencies of government, to voluntarily undertake efforts to remedy conspicuous racial imbalances in the work force. In his majority opinion Justice Brennan implicitly contrasted this type of affirmative action with other plans which were imposed, mandated, and required by governmental agencies and public institutions such as courts of law. This contrast could only appeal to those traditionally opposed to governmental regulation of private business; presumably this kind of argument could also persuade Supreme Court justices sympathetic to a jurisprudence of judicial restraint. The Kaiser plan could pass muster because it was voluntarily agreed to by management and labor and therefore involved respect for "management prerogatives and union freedoms."

In the *Weber* case, the Court rejected Brian Weber's interpretation of Title VII as absolutely prohibiting all forms of discrimination based on race. The Court's message in *Weber* was a bit clearer than it had been in *Bakke*. Justice Brennan in the majority opinion stressed that Kaiser's voluntary compliance with the overall purpose of the Civil Rights Act should be encouraged. Employers should voluntarily and flexibly remedy past discrimination rather than wait for courts and other federal agencies to compel such action.

A year later, the Court handed down another major ruling on affirmative action in *Fullilove* v. *Klutznick*. In contrast to *Weber,* which concerned programs of preferential treatment voluntarily undertaken by parties in the private sector, *Fullilove* involved the kinds of racial preferences which could be required by institutions in the public sector (in this case Congress). The case concerned a $4 billion public works program enacted by Congress in 1977 which stipulated that a fixed percentage—10 percent—of all federal contracts be set aside for minority construction firms.[20]

The fixed 10 percent set-aside requirement was promptly challenged in fifteen lawsuits around the country by trade associations representing nonminority construction companies. *Fullilove* was the first of these cases to reach a federal appeals court. In 1979 the Court of Appeals for the Second Circuit upheld the set-aside provision as a valid exercise of congressional power. Four associations of construction firms in New York State then appealed to the Supreme Court.

The question before the Court was whether Congress had the authority to enact a set-aside program to remedy the effects of past discrimination in the construction industry. In a six-to-three decision the Court upheld this congressionally enacted affirmative action program.[21] Affirming the lower court rulings, Chief Justice Burger's opinion held that Congress possessed both a factual basis for concluding that minority contractors had suffered from discrimination and the constitutional authority to remedy the problem. "We reject the contention that in the remedial context the Congress must act in a wholly 'color-blind' fashion," Burger wrote. "It is fundamental that in no organ of government, state or Federal, does there repose a more comprehensive remedial power than in the Congress, which is expressly charged by the Constitution with competence and authority to enforce equal protection guarantees."

The chief justice concluded that "the limited use of racial and ethnic criteria, in the context presented, is a constitutionally permissible means" for achieving the congressional objectives of promoting equality of economic opportunity. In an explicit endorsement of Congress's awarding of federal benefits on the basis of race, Burger stated, "The Congress has not sought to give selective minority groups a preferred standing in the construction industry, but has embarked on a remedial program to place them on a more equitable footing with respect to public contracting opportunities."

Justice Thurgood Marshall, in a concurring opinion, stated that it was "indisputable that Congress's articulated purpose for enacting the set-aside provision was to remedy the present effects of past racial discrimination." In an eloquent passage Marshall reiterated the fundamental rationale for affirmative action: "By upholding this race-conscious remedy, the Court accords Congress the authority to undertake the task of moving our society toward a state of meaningful equality of opportunity, not an abstract version of equality in which the effects of past discrimination would be forever frozen into our social fabric. I applaud this result."

Coming two years after the ambiguous opinions in the *Bakke* case and one year after the carefully crafted statutory ruling in the *Weber* case, the Court's decision in *Fullilove* gave renewed legal and political momentum to affirmative action. The six justices in the majority clearly accepted the essential premise of affirmative action: not only does the Constitution permit race-consciousness in pursuit of the goal of equal economic opportunity, colorblindness is inadequate when disadvantaged groups have to catch up to compete fairly. In its acceptance of this premise, *Fullilove* has provided a powerful constitutional statement which could become a potent instrument for minorities seeking genuine equality of opportunity in American society. Proponents of affirmative action may well find in this opinion the support they sought—and did not get—from the court in *Bakke*. *Fullilove* broadens the impact of the *Weber* ruling and relegates *Bakke* to relative obscurity. Whereas *Bakke* and *Weber* may be remembered for the public debate and controversy they occasioned, *Fullilove* may have far greater economic and social consequences.

Nevertheless, *Fullilove* does not completely put to rest the matter of the legality of affirmative action. According to Linda Greenhouse, the *New York Times's* Supreme Court reporter, some important questions still to be resolved are these:

(1) Assuming that a race-based remedy for discrimination is permissible, how should the remedy be designed? What is a valid "target"? If a 10 percent set-aside is acceptable, what about 30 percent?

(2) Is it constitutional to take away someone's vested right or legitimate expectation in the name of creating new opportunity for someone else?

(C) When does a policy that distinguishes among racial groups for the purpose of a "benign" remedy cross the barrier and become invidious, and therefore unconstitutional, racial discrimination?[22]

In its 1980-81 term the Court had an opportunity in two cases to resolve some of these questions. In *Minnick* v. *California Department of Corrections* two white male corrections officers challenged California's affirmative action plan designed to increase the number of women and minorities among California prison personnel. The goals were 38 percent women and 35 percent racial minorities. In the second case, *Johnson* v. *Board of Education,* several black students challenged the Chicago school board which, in order to stabilize the racial composition of schools in transitional neighborhoods, turned black students away from two local high schools to preserve a fifty-fifty racial balance. This second case was to test the outer limits of the distinction between benign and invidious discrimination.

By the end of the 1980-81 term, the Court had dismissed these two cases as moot or procedurally defective. The Chicago case was dismissed because the city had entered into an agreement with the U.S. Justice Department to devise a new desegregation plan that might possibly resolve the problem without further court intervention. *Minnick* v. *California Department of Corrections* was dismissed on the grounds that ambiguities in the record and the need for further lower court proceedings to clarify the actual effect of the plan had made it impossible for the Supreme Court to decide the merits of the case. Thus lingering questions about the outer constitutional limits of governmental policies based on race remain to be resolved.

In this chapter we have reviewed the legal bases for affirmative action, ranging from congressional statutes and executive orders to recent important rulings by the Supreme Court. The legal validity of affirmative action now seems firmly grounded, even if further clarification is required. Nevertheless, the morality of affirmative action—its justice or fairness—is still the subject of heated controversy. In the next chapter we shall examine the moral grounds for affirmative action.

6

Justifying Affirmative Action

Mary C. Segers

> If moves toward an egalitarian society are to be serious they must
> include abolishing privilege, especially as it places certain children
> on an inside track.
>
> **Andrew Hacker**
> *Creating American Inequality*

Affirmative action is among the most controversial of American political
issues. Given the real short-term costs and the equally real but longer-run benefits
of affirmative action, it is legitimate to ask how and why the policy may be
justified. Does American society have an obligation to take special steps to end
present racial and sex-based discrimination and to ensure that groups previously
discriminated against no longer suffer the ill effects of past discrimination? Few
would contest the first part of this obligation; that is, few would argue that society
ought to acquiesce passively in the face of ongoing racial and sexual discrimination. However, many citizens do question whether society and government should make special efforts on behalf of women and minorities in order to
offset the pervasive effects of past discrimination. Why, many ask, should special
attention and preferential treatment be accorded women, blacks, and other
minorities in the competition for jobs and places in American society? Does not
attention to these individuals and groups mean inattention to others? If so, how
can such differential treatment be justified?

In the years since current affirmative action requirements were stated in 1965, a
number of justifications have been advanced. These arguments on behalf of
preferential treatment for women and minorities may be classified into three
broad categories: appeals to principles of compensatory justice; appeals to the
principle of utility; and egalitarian arguments stressing the primacy of a liberal
democratic society's obligation to ensure genuine equality of opportunity to all.
Compensatory or retrospective justifications of preferential treatment focus on
the historical past and argue that affirmative action is necessary to compensate

women and minorities for past injustices and/or for present disadvantages stemming from past injustices. Utilitarian arguments stress the benefits to individuals and to society as a whole of having members of previously disadvantaged groups in business and the professions. Finally, egalitarian justifications stress the importance of affirmative action as a means of realizing genuine equality of opportunity for all individuals in the present and future regardless of utility. Whether such equality contributes to individual or social welfare is an important but not essential consideration. The central point is the equal dignity of every person which, in the liberal theory of equality, implies equality before the law and equality of opportunity in social life.

To some extent, of course, these three justifications may overlap. While appeals to compensatory justice are heavily retrospective, they are also prospective; that is, they look to the present and the future. Similarly, it may be difficult to defend the right in principle of every person to equal employment opportunity without stressing the benefits or utilities to the individual and to society which greater vocational chances will bring in terms of prosperity, self-fulfillment, productivity, and general well-being. These examples should indicate how difficult it is to compartmentalize the types of arguments used to justify affirmative action. Nevertheless, for purposes of clarity it is useful to isolate and identify these three main arguments which have appeared recurrently in the relatively short history of public debate over affirmative action.

Before discussing the historical development and philosophical cogency of arguments justifying affirmative action, it is important to be clear—once again—on exactly what it is that is being justified. Broadly speaking, affirmative action refers to measures and programs which are sensitive to and take cognizance of factors of race, sex, or national origin in admissions, hiring, and promotion decisions.[1] Such measures include remedial training programs, validation of employment and admissions tests, and broad advertising and recruitment efforts in order to alert women and minorities to school and job opportunities. There is relatively little public discussion of the justice or morality of these particular measures, although employers have been known to complain of the additional costs of advertising and remedial training programs. Rather, the controversy over affirmative action has centered on whether the use of numerical goals and timetables for increasing the representation of women and minorities in the work force implies sacrificing principles of merit and diluting standards of quality in order to meet these established targets.

While affirmative action is *not* synonymous with quotas, it does require that, where necessary, special consideration be given to women, blacks and minorities. The policy thus raises a fundamental question: can differential, and preferential, treatment of women and minorities in educational and employment opportunities be justified? We shall consider next the three answers to this question that were noted above: defending affirmative action through an appeal to the principle of equality of opportunity, through an appeal to principles of utility, and on grounds of compensatory justice.

In general, a liberal conception of society will invoke the principle of merit to explain and justify social inequalities and the equal opportunity principle to explain and justify equality. For a number of years now, however, the doctrine of equality of opportunity has been the subject of considerable controversy. Roughly stated, the equal opportunity principle suggests the importance of the absence of arbitrary restrictions on access to jobs or positions, where "arbitrary" means irrelevant to success or performance in the work. As John Schaar has noted in what has come to be regarded as a classic exposition and critique of the equal opportunity doctrine,[2] the formula is attractive *precisely because* it takes full account of natural differences and does not assume that human beings are in fact equal. With this built-in tolerance for diversity and its implied justification for liberty to capitalize upon diversity, the equal opportunity principle is indeed an appropriate part of a liberal political theory. The doctrine has not been without its critics, however. It has been faulted as an inherently conservative principle which operates to reinforce the established values and structure of an ongoing society and offers no challenge to the status quo. Others have argued that equality of opportunity is (1) impossible to achieve, given natural and environmental differences among humans;[3] (2) impossible to achieve because it requires programs which are too costly and represent excessive governmental intervention in the workings of a free enterprise economy;[4] and (3) impossible to maintain, assuming it could ever be achieved.[5]

This is not the place to engage in an extended discussion of the merits and deficiencies of the liberal equal opportunity formula. For our purposes here we need only have a working definition of the doctrine, and for that purpose we shall take John Schaar's formulation: "The principle of equality of opportunity asserts that each man should have equal rights and opportunities to develop his own talents and virtues and that there should be equal rewards for equal performances."[6]

In the 1960s this doctrine was used to justify a variety of public policies and programs ranging from the so-called "War on Poverty" to federal aid to elementary and secondary education. Both the 1964 Civil Rights Act and the 1965 Executive Order 11246 requiring affirmative action of federal contractors were justified as necessary to overcome the residual effects of de jure and de facto segregation and to give real meaning to the idea of equal opportunity. In defending affirmative action, President Johnson—in a 1965 commencement speech at Howard University—stressed the primacy of a liberal democratic society's obligations to ensure genuine equality of opportunity to all as a means of enhancing individual liberty:

Freedom is not enough. You do not wipe out scars of centuries by saying, "Now you're free to go where you want and do as you desire." You do not take a person who for years has been hobbled by chains and liberate him, bring him up to the starting line of a race, and then say "You're free to compete" and justly believe you have been completely fair. Thus it is not enough to open the gates to opportunity. All of our citizens must have the ability to walk through those gates; and this is the next and the most profound stage of the battle for civil rights.[7]

As suggested in Johnson's speech, an image frequently employed by policy-makers to justify affirmative action was that of the shackled runner:

Imagine a hundred-yard dash in which one of the two runners has his legs shackled together. He has progressed ten yards, while the unshackled runner has gone fifty yards. At that point the judges decide that the race is unfair. How do they rectify the situation? Do they merely remove the shackles and allow the race to proceed? Then they could say that "equal opportunity" now prevailed. But one of the runners would still be forty yards ahead of the other. Would it not be the better part of justice to allow the previously shackled runner to make up the forty-yard gap, or to start the race all over again? That would be affirmative action toward equality.[8]

Such imagery captures well the competitive ethic guiding many activities and enterprises in this liberal-capitalist society. In such a society the equal opportunity formula is one of the principles governing fair competition. As J. L. Lucas states: "The principle has a limited, subordinate, but perfectly respectable part to play in the structure of competitions, where it serves as a standard for criticism of rules or factors which confer advantages or impose disadvantages not connected with the main purpose of the competition."[9] In the name of genuine equality of opportunity, then, one could criticize those factors which impose disadvantages upon minorities in the struggle for jobs and places in society, and one could institute remedial programs and undertake special efforts to remove the disabilities stemming from past discrimination. Moreover, as the image of the foot race suggests, one might handicap previously unshackled runners, thereby giving members of historically disadvantaged groups an edge in the process of competition.

Giving them this advantage, however, would be admittedly risky, since it seems to constitute a departure from the very principle it was intended to promote. How could one achieve meaningful equality of opportunity through affirmative action policies which denied the very principle they were designed to realize? From the start, affirmative action in general and preferential treatment in particular appeared problematic and posed the logical and practical dilemma: can one deny equal opportunity to some in order to realize it for others? From the beginning it seemed that the equal opportunity principle in itself was insufficient to justify affirmative action and that recourse to other justificatory principles would be necessary.

Utilitarian justifications of affirmative action stress the benefits to individuals and to society as a whole of having members of previously disadvantaged groups in business and the professions. Typically such appeals to social utility emphasize the importance of having black and female professionals as role models for the young. Also stressed is the educational value of having women and minority students in professional schools to present their viewpoints and otherwise act as a leavening force in the training of future professionals for a pluralistic society. A third utilitarian argument justifies using preferential policies to increase educational and employment opportunities as a means of promoting the public welfare by eliminating poverty and its attendant evils and by eliminating the sort of economic inequality that leads to resentment and strife. Extreme poverty and even the economic inequality we currently suffer—with wide gaps of income and wealth and with some groups perennially concentrated at the bottom of the economic ladder—is said to be objectionable because of what it involves or may lead to: unmet human needs causing suffering, crime, family disintegration, lack of self-respect, social discontent, and possibly political instability.[10] Still a fourth connection between utility and the use of affirmative action is found in the need of disadvantaged minorities for persons who can and will provide them with legal and medical services. Thomas Nagel explores this connection:

> Suppose for example that there is a need for a great increase in the number of black doctors, because the health needs of the black community are unlikely to be met otherwise. And suppose that at the present average level of premedical qualifications among black applicants, it would require a huge expansion of total medical school enrollment to supply the desirable absolute number of black doctors without adopting differential admissions standards. Such an expansion may be unacceptable either because of its cost or because it would produce a total supply of doctors, black and white, much greater than society requires. This is a strong argument for accepting reverse discrimination, not on grounds of justice but on grounds of social utility.[11]

A utilitarian analysis of the grounds for policies of affirmative action and preferential treatment will stress these benefits said to flow from the use of such policies. But such an analysis will also calculate the costs and risks of such practices. We are all too familiar with what these include: (1) inevitable resentment among those better qualified, who are passed over because of the policy; (2) resentment even among those in the discriminated-against group (i.e., white males) who would in fact have failed to gain a desired position in any case on the basis of their qualifications, but who are now allowed to feel that they may have lost out to someone less qualified simply because of their race or sex;[12] (3) a negative effect stigmatizing as inferior those admitted or hired as a result of the preferential policy;[13] (4) threats to the self-esteem of those in the preferred groups who would in fact have gained their positions even in the absence of the preferential practices, but who cannot be sure that they are not among its beneficiaries;[14] and (5) the risk of an increase rather than a decrease in racial consciousness and racial tensions. These costs cannot be evaded or ignored. Utilitarian advocates of affirmative action and preferential policies must take them into account and must plausibly claim that they are outweighed by greater benefits. As is the case with all consequential arguments such as the utilitarian's, strong reliance upon empirical data concerning the actual practice and results of affirmative action is imperative.

Additionally, utilitarian advocates of affirmative action and preferential policies must consider that, as George Sher remarked, "The winds of utilitarian argumentation blow in too many directions."[15] What is socially useful changes over time; and what is considered socially beneficial and of high priority at one point may, given changes in political administration or changes in the economy, assume less importance and less urgency than in a previous period. In fact, a fate very similar to just this has befallen some affirmative action programs which have succumbed to political changes as well as to the pressures of budgetary retrenchment in the wake of the recessionary periods of 1974-75 and the contemporary austerity. In the face of a shift from an expanding to a contracting economy, the attention of some employers must inevitably be focused on holding the line rather than upon increasing the numbers of minorities and women in the work force. Thus utilitarian proponents of affirmative action must not only balance competing utilities, but must constantly monitor particular facts and cases in changing circumstances and be prepared to modify their position accordingly. Such flexibility does not seem to afford very firm grounding for what many consider matters of right and justice.

A more telling argument against utilitarian justifications of affirmative action, however, concerns the balancing of individual rights against social utilities. An individual may be said to have a right, when applying for a position, not to be discriminated against on the basis of race but rather to be judged on his or her merit. Can this right be overridden by social policy which promises greater benefits for the general welfare in the long term? Are we here presented with yet another instance of the utilitarian's weakness in the matter of defending individual rights, the kind of weakness which John Rawls notes in his comparison of utilitarianism with his notion of "justice and fairness"? Writes Rawls:

It has seemed to many philosophers, and it appears to be supported by the convictions of common sense, that we distinguish as a matter of principle between the claims of liberty and right on the one hand and the desirability of increasing aggregate social welfare on the other; and that we give a certain priority, if not absolute weight, to the former. Each member of society is thought to have an inviolability founded on justice or, as some say, on natural right, which even the welfare of everyone else cannot override. Justice denies that the loss of freedom for some is made right by a greater good shared by others.[16]

If this intuition concerning the inviolability of individual rights supports the white male who might be passed over by preferential policies, it also lends support to the position of those (women and minorities) who defend reverse discrimination as a matter of individual right to just compensation for past injustices. As Sher puts it: "To rest a defense of reverse discrimination upon utilitarian considerations would be to ignore what is surely the guiding intuition of its proponents, that this treatment is *deserved* where discrimination has been practiced in the past. It is the intuition that reverse discrimination is a matter not (only) of social good but of right...."[17]

Utilitarian arguments about the benefits of various social policies to the common welfare must eventually yield to considerations of individual rights and of how to balance two such rights: "the entitlement of every American to be judged on his or her merits when applying for a position without regard to race, sex or creed; and the legitimate claim of hitherto disadvantaged groups to be compensated for at least part of their past losses."[18] We turn next to examine the notion of compensatory justice which underlies the defense of affirmative action as a means of creating genuine equality of opportunity and which is invoked whenever utilitarian justifications of affirmative action begin to crumble in the face of changing social circumstances.

The principle of compensatory justice says that "anyone who causes an injury to an innocent other owes rectification of that injury."[19] The practice of seeking in courts of law redress for losses or injuries sustained is a familiar notion of compensatory justice in modern society. Like many important legal and political ideas, however, the idea of compensatory justice has a long lineage, and may be traced to Aristotle's classic discussion of justice in book 5 of the *Nicomachean Ethics.* There Aristotle distinguished corrective justice, which plays a rectifying role in transactions between individuals, from distributive justice, which concerns the division of offices, honors, money, or other goods among the citizens of a state. According to Aristotle, corrective justice obtains in both voluntary transactions (commercial intercourse such as loans and sales) and involuntary transactions (such as theft, assassination, assault, murder).[20] Common to both voluntary and involuntary transactions involving corrective justice is (1) an undeserved injury, (2) deliberately inflicted by one party upon the other, (3) of undeserved benefit to the party causing the injury, (4) which results in an imbalance calling for rectification, by taking from the offender something appropriate to make up to the victim for his loss, thereby restoring the equilibrium of the *status quo ante* between them.[21] In such instances, Aristotle maintained, the law looks only to the difference created by the injury and treats the two people as previously equal (that is, the law does not permit the poor person in great need to rob the rich person living in the lap of luxury). The judge seeks to remove the arithmetic inequality that has been introduced into their relationship and to restore the *status quo ante* by imposing a penalty upon the offender equal to the gain that he has illegitimately obtained.

The two branches of corrective justice identified by Aristotle are today dealt with under law in quite distinct ways. Voluntary transactions involving commercial dealings subject to, for example, breach of contrct are the subject of long-standing social interest in private suits for civil damages (including restitution or monetary compensation). Involuntary actions constitute what we call criminal offenses, which are generally dealt with by punishing the criminal offender but not necessarily by recompensing the victim of the crime. It is only in recent years that we have come to accept the notion of victim compensation schemes paid out of the public treasury.[22] The purpose of such schemes is to restore the victim's losses of money or property, and/or to provide compensation for loss of life, physical injury (with consequent loss of earning power and the cost of medical care), and the pain and suffering resulting from criminal assaults.[23]

Still another form of compensation is the category of tort law, that is, compensation for injuries that are neither violation of a contract nor commission of a crime but that occur through culpable negligence or even through accident, mistake, or ignorance. While Aristotle does not mention torts, modern society has long agreed that it has an interest in imposing liability on those whose conduct failed to measure up to some standard of reasonable care. The assumption is that compensatory justice has to be concerned not only with malicious injuries but also with injuries to the innocent that arise from no motive or intention; all such injuries need to be rectified.[24]

The particular conditions specified by Aristotle in situations of compensatory justice—namely, that corrective justice concerns transactions between individuals in which one party has deliberately injured another innocent party, and in so doing has profited or gained unfairly at the other's expense, and must therefore make recompense to the injured party—these conditions have under today's law been stretched considerably. Under tort law, injuries need not be inflicted deliberately with malicious intent. Under no-fault automobile insurance systems, compensation for injury and loss is emphasized while individual culpability is downplayed, and the cost of compensation is spread out among all members of the insurance plan. In the field of criminal justice, victim compensation schemes employ public funds extracted from the taxpayers on the grounds that the state, in the person of its police force, has failed to perform its duty of protecting the citizenry. In these ways there has occurred erosion of the Aristotelian notions of individual accountability and individual responsibility to bear the costs of compensating injuried parties.

How does this apparent digression bear upon justification of affirmative action? It is important to understand the bases of compensatory justice because, given its deep-seated place in Western culture, even our modified legal and moral thinking on the subject of one party's compensating losses and injuries caused another party led perhaps inevitably to appeals to notions of compensatory justice to justify affirmative action. Since the 1960s, current events as well as articles in journals of law and philosophy have called to the public's attention the question whether the white majority of contemporary American society had a duty to compensate the black minority for centuries of discrimination and exploitation. The claim was made most publicly and forcefully in May, 1969, when James Foreman interrupted a religious service at Riverside Church in New York City to deliver "The Black Manifesto," which called for $500 million dollars in "reparations" to be paid to black Americans by the white religious establishment. This stunning demand triggered a spate of articles in journals of political commentary and philosophical analysis. Perhaps the most serious book-length analysis of the argument that American blacks as a whole be compensated for past discrimination was made by a lawyer, Professor Boris Bittker, in *The Case for Black Reparations,* published in 1973.[25] Pointing to the example of the Federal Compensation Law under which West Germany paid reparations to Nazi victims, Bittker explored the factual basis (slavery and postemancipation conditions of blacks in America) for racial redress, analyzed the problem of individual versus collective liability, discussed what might be an appropriate amount of compensation, and considered the legal basis for such a demand by black Americans. Bittker acknowledged the legal difficulties a court would encounter in adjudicating any such claim,[26] but held out hope for a congressionally enacted program of black reparations which could be validated (if that became necessary) through a constitutional amendment.

Given the political controversy generated by the U.S. Supreme Court's hearing of the *Bakke* case, Professor Bittker's hope for legislative enactment of a program of black reparations seems futile indeed. Moreover, Bittker's citation of the Jewish case as valid precedent for payment of compensation to living descendents of slaves in America seems incorrect. In the German case victims were compensated for *personal* loss of freedom during incarceration in concentration camps. Such compensation did not extend to the children of Jewish survivors unless they also had been imprisoned. Compensation for loss of previously owned property was made only on condition that Holocaust victims or their immediate heirs submit substantial proof of ownership. Given these strict definitions and conditions, the Jewish case would not seem to set much of a precedent for blacks hoping to be compensated for suffering imposed on ancestors in the distant past. As one commentator remarked, "If the method of compensating Jewish survivors of the Holocaust were to be applied to the present generation of American blacks, not one black person would get a single penny."[27]

Despite those modern legal developments (tort law, no-fault insurance, victim compensation schemes) which have tended to deemphasize the notion of individual responsibility as a prerequisite for compensation, there are serious problems with arguments that the white majority of *present* American society must provide compensation for injuries and wrongs done by their ancestors to blacks in the *past*. There is, first, the theoretical and practical problem of how far this principle of compensation for past discrimination should be extended. Are there any logical grounds for distinguishing blacks and women, say, from the many other ethnic, racial, and religious groups in American society who might also point to past discrimination and, presumably, also claim that they deserve compensation? Given the broad character of past discrimination against many, if not most, newly arrived immigrants, we might wonder which residual group would be left to pay the compensation.

An even more serious set of objections arises when we consider that the idea of compensatory justice involves corollary notions of collective responsibility and societal guilt. The notion that society as a whole or a majority of its members must compensate for past injuries to a minority makes no distinction between white civil rights workers and white advocates of racial supremacy. Similarly, among the minority to be compensated, no distinction is drawn between those who are seriously disadvantaged and needy and those (perhaps relatively few) who have achieved high levels of status, income, and wealth. It is assumed that all minority members have themselves been discriminated against and have been injured to the same extent. Such notions do not account for the differential impact of discrimination on the members of a group (whether black, female, or Hispanic).

Finally, current arguments for compensatory justice assume a notion of intergenerational (collective) responsibility which seems to violate our sense of fairness and equity. Under the rubric of compensatory justice, people (especially white males) are linked to deeds with which they have had no proximate or volitional connection. As Herbert Deane states:

Present members of the society are being asked to assume the responsibility not only for unjust acts in the present or the recent past in which they may have had no share, but also for acts of discrimination which were performed long before they were born, and when, indeed, their fathers and grandfathers may not have been Americans at all but may have been suffering persecution and discrimination, for example, in Eastern Europe. We are, in other words, asked to accept not merely the principle of collective guilt but also the even more distasteful notion of collective guilt that is at least in part inherited from some of the ancestors of some contemporary Americans.[28]

In the debate about affirmative action, advocates of preferential treatment on grounds of compensatory justice have responded to some of these criticisms by appealing to administrative convenience and by attempting to distinguish among those groups which have suffered past discrimination. With respect to the overinclusive nature of preferential treatment in compensating all members of a racial category whether advantaged or disadvantaged, defenders of compensatory justice point to the extraordinary difficulty in fashioning a remedy on an individual or case-by-case basis. As the solicitor-general argued in the *Bakke* case:

Decades of discrimination by public bodies and private persons may have far-reaching effects that make it difficult for minority applicants to compete...on an equal basis. The consequences of discrimination are too complex to dissect case-by-case; the effects on aspirations alone may raise for minority applicants a hurdle that does not face white applicants...and a [school or employer] dealing with imponderables of this sort ought not to be confined to the choice of either ignoring the problem or attempting the Sisyphean task of discerning its importance on an individual basis.[29]

With respect to the logical difficulty of distinguishing among those groups (racial, ethnic, sexual, religious) which have suffered past discrimination and might therefore be deserving of compensation, defenders of compensatory justice have advanced historical arguments as to why only some groups should be compensated. Blacks and women are said to have suffered legal as well as social discrimination while, for example, Irish and Italian immigrants suffered only the latter. Blacks under slavery were regarded as chattel, were nonpersons in the eyes of the law, and were denied citizenship and the right to vote; women were denied legal rights to own property and were also denied the right to vote. In these cases it was the state through its legal system which publicly accorded members of these groups second-class status. In the case of discrimination against ethnic or religious groups, it was society which discriminated in nonpublic, private relationships. As Earl Rabb has written:

An assignable act of atrocity was committed against the American blacks by this society: they were brought here and enslaved. An assignable act of atrocity was committed against the American Indians by this society. In both cases, the group oppression was so total, and so assignable to this society, and the consequences for the present generation so apparent, that it is a legitimate if unusual piece of enlightenment for this society to try to provide some special group-oriented remedy, some affirmative action that stays within the basic structures of democratic life. Other current underprivileged population groups came here voluntarily, often from even less privileged positions. They have also been treated badly and in a discriminatory fashion here, and society does owe them equal treatment and equal opportunity on every level; but it does not owe then the same historic debt it owes the American blacks and Indians.[30]

Despite the distinctions and the appeals to administrative convenience put forth by advocates of a compensatory approach to affirmative action, it seems difficult to defend the idea that contemporary American society or a majority thereof owes compensation to a minority for wrongs done in the historical past. Intuitively most Americans today would disclaim responsibility for slavery and for post-Civil War Jim Crow practices. To rest the case for affirmative action and preferential treatment on some vague notion of collective guilt and a social duty to pay recompense for wrongs committed by ancestors who lived long ago seems unnecessary and misguided. It is unnecessary because, as we will indicate in greater detail below, affirmative action may be more effectively defended through appeals to distributive justice and fair equality of opportunity. It is misguided because basing affirmative action on notions of compensatory justice is likely to alienate dominant, established groups in society and is unlikely to win the requisite political support for such programs. For these reasons, some have argued that it is both more intellectually defensible and politically realistic to view current claims by minorities for compensatory justice as claims involving new or revised principles of distributive justice.[31]

This does not mean that the history of groups which have suffered flagrant discrimination in the past is irrelevant. What it does mean is that the obligation to ensure genuine equality of opportunity to members of groups who have been historically disadvantaged is rooted in contemporary society's commitment to create a more just distributionn of goods. On this view, programs using preferential policies are conceived as a means of promoting the redistributio of income and other important benefits in the name of distributive justice. A concern with distributive justice is a concern with whether people have fair shares of benefits and burdens. Given the present distribution of income and wealth and the concentration of certain groups on the lower rungs of the economic ladder,[32] the use of special opportunities to offset disadvantages stemming from past injustice may be justified as a means of achieving a society in which all individuals have more equitable shares of the benefits and burdens of American life.

Compensatory programs differ from distributive programs mainly in regard to their concern with the past. While redistribution is concerned with eliminating present inequities, compensatory justice is concerned not only with this but with providing compensation for unfair burdens borne in the past. Few deny the relevance of the history of women and minorities in the United States; the past is important in identifying historically disadvantaged groups and in partially explaining the results of statistical and sociological analyses of the contemporary work force and of the current maldistribution of wealth, income, and status in the nation. But one need not rest the case for special policies to help the disadvantaged on illusory notions of an obligation on the part of the present generation to compensate for burdens imposed and borne in the past. Rather, as George Sher puts it, "It is the key to an adequate justification of reverse discrimination to see that practice, not as the redressing of *past* deprivations, but rather as a way of neutralizing the *present* competitive disadvantage caused by those past privations and thus as a way of restoring equal access to those goods which society distributes competitively."[33]

The difference between "redressing past privations" and "neutralizing the present competitive disadvantage" stemming from past privations is not merely semantic. As Nickel has stressed, depending on the argument used (to justify affirmative action and preferential treatment), different groups will benefit from preferential policies, and racial, ethnic, and sexual classifications will be used with greater or lesser defensibility.[34] In justifying affirmative action, reliance upon an appeal to distributive justice and to fair equality of opportunity would obviate the necessity of accepting the group classifications inherent in the compensatory justice approach. The claims of the poor white from Appalachia or of the individual from a lower-middle class ethnic group would not automatically be ruled out of consideration. Such an approach, in rejecting the use of race as a criterion and substituting a concern with economic and cultural disadvantage, would be a more precise and accurate instrument of social justice.

On the other hand, there is some reason to believe that reliance upon a colorblind approach based on economic disadvantage would not materially alter the proportion of minorities in professional schools, for example, and would simply perpetuate the status quo. A study prepared for the nation's law schools found that, had the schools adhered to a racially neutral admissions policy, only one in five black students admitted for the 1976-77 academic year would have been accepted.[35] When we consider that, at every rung of the income ladder, there are more whites than blacks or Spanish-speaking minorities, and that the last decade has witnessed an enormous increase in applicants for the limited number of places in American professional schools, we are probably justified in concluding that the use of economic rather than racial criteria for preferential treatment would have no significant impact upon the disproportionate representation of blacks and minorities in the low income groups of American society. Thus, the use of racial criteria would seem necessary in order adequately to assist those who have suffered the double disadvantage of poverty and racism—however the two may be related—and in order thereby to achieve a more equitable distribution of jobs and places in American society.

We have said that the equal opportunity principle in itself did not justify affirmative action and preferential treatment because such policies seemed to deny equal access to some individuals in order to guarantee it to others. Similarly, principles of utility seemed to provide strong justification of affirmative action—only to meet with strong counterclaims of social disutility. Appeals to compensatory justice have seemed unsatisfactory because they impute to society the notion of collective guilt, they assume responsibility across generations, and they rely too heavily upon group classifications which are more blunt than precise. Given these objections to current arguments for affirmative action, is it possible to outline a defensible justification of the policy?

It is possible to suggest what elements an adequate justification might include. Affirmative action and preferential treatment may be justified primarily through an appeal to notions of distributive justice and genuine equality of opportunity supplemented by elements drawn from utilitarian arguments and theories of compensatory justice. Such an approach would distinguish between preferential treatment to correct *present* inequities stemming from past injustices and the less defensible argument for preferential treatment by the present generation to compensate for unfair burdens imposed and borne in the past.[36] A plausible and defensible justification of affirmative action and preferential treatment will:

(1) be partially meritocratic in insisting upon minimum qualifications for jobs and positions in education and employment.[37] (This departs from the idea that the

most qualified, as measured solely by conventional criteria, should automatically be preferred.) The criterion of merit must be retained partly in recognition of the principle that effort and talent must be rewarded. The application of meritocratic criteria must be tempered, however, by the recognition that intelligence. motivation, ambition, and the desire to expend effort are often functions of forces and circumstances (such as natural inheritance and social environment) which are currently beyond human control and therefore appear arbitrary from a moral point of view;

(2) incorporate but not rely wholly and completely upon utilitarian arguments and considerations regarding the advantages to be derived from increased representation of women and minorities in the professions and institutions of higher education;

(3) take as its point of departure a critique of society based upon principles of distributive justice—what might be considered a fair share of society's benefits and burdens. Statistical analyses of distribution curves of income and wealth in contemporary American society must be considered in the light of theoretical models of an ideally just society (such as that of Rawls, or chapter 9, for example);

(4) be directed primarily toward transforming what Rawls has termed formal equality of opportunity into fair equality of opportunity. It should be noted that (3) and (4) are two separate goals: given the limitations of the equal opportunity principle, realizing fair equality of opportunity means giving everyone an equal chance to be unequal. But achieving ever closer approximations to distributive justice may mean overhauling the structure of occupational rewards in capitalist American society (see, for example, some of the suggestions made in chapter 9). Benjamin Ringer argues that affirmative action, as presently constituted, does not so much challenge the structure of occupational reward as simply try to make it work equally for members of all groups in society;[38]

(5) regard the historical past as relevant insofar as past discrimination and injustice influences present ability to compete for social goods. The historical past is useful in identifying members of those groups most likely to need assistance and in partly explaining the results of statistical analyses which reveal wide disparities in income, status, and wealth. An adequate justification of affirmative action will accept the relevance of the past but will not argue that the present generation has a duty to pay for, or should have visited upon them, the sins of its fathers. A sound affirmative action approach would distinguish between compensating for unfair burdens imposed and borne in the past and neutralizing present disadvantages stemming from past injustices. Such an approach would permit the use of race-sensitive and sex-sensitive measures, together with other factors, in employment and admissions. It would thereby incorporate one of the requirements of justice—that treating persons as equals may sometimes mean that we must treat them differently.

7

Evaluating Affirmative Action: The Limitations of Redistributional Politics in Achieving Equality

Mary C. Segers

> People who are outraged by affirmative action must have thought they once lived in a utopia, where only qualified people were admitted to schools and professions.
>
> **Esther Hyneman**
> *New York Times,* **July 26, 1980**

Thus far we have examined the *legality* of affirmative action through analysis of recent important Supreme Court decisions concerning equal opportunity in education and employment. In the chapter immediately preceding, we discussed the *morality* of affirmative action by examining the three major types of argument advanced to justify this policy. It is time now to come to some conclusions regarding the effectiveness of this policy. Affirmative action is a public policy designed to remedy unjust inequalities in American society. It has been in operation for at least fifteen years now. Are its promises realized? Has it brought about greater equality of opportunity in the United States? Can we point to specific victories and defeats in its short history? More importantly, what does affirmative action tell us about our society? In what ways does this policy exemplify strengths and weaknesses of the prevailing liberal conception of equality?

In evaluating affirmative action, we shall examine briefly some of its successes, then analyze some of the recurring difficulties in administering this policy. Finally, we shall discuss why affirmative action's potential for achieving greater equality has not been realized. The reasons for this have less to do with the policy itself; they relate more to flaws in the very notion of equality of opportunity—proprietary equality—and to deficiencies in the very structure of a mature liberal-capitalist society. The reduction of inequality in the United States, we shall eventually argue, depends upon rethinking our conception of equality and upon fundamental structural changes in our political economy.

In general, statistics concerning progress made under affirmative action programs are unavailable. Indeed, as we noted in chapter 5, there is little hard empirical evidence to support either charges of reverse discrimination made by white males or assertions that significant progress toward the elimination of systemic patterns of race- and sex-based discrimination has resulted from affirmative action policies. In the absence of empirical data, one is forced to rely upon impressionistic accounts and individual case studies of affirmative action.

At the same time, census data is available which shows that, in aggregate terms, the situation of blacks and of women in American society has not improved over the last fifteen years. There is a persistence of occupational segregation in the work force, with women being concentrated in low-paying service ("pink-collar") jobs while men are overrepresented in high-paying executive positions. There is also the persistence of income differentials between men and women and between blacks and whites. In 1978, the last year (as of this writing) for which figures are available, the median salary for women working full time was only 59 percent of that of men, and working women with college degrees earned, on the average, less than men with an eighth-grade education.[1] The statistics with respect to blacks are no more encouraging. Since 1968, for example, the median income of black families has remained forty percentage points behind the white figure (it has ranged from a high of 61 percent in 1969 to a low of 57 percent in 1977).[2] It would seem that the "opportunity" given to blacks has been to move ahead so long as they keep their distance behind whites. For blacks as a whole and for women as a whole, then, it may be the case that affirmative action has not made much progress in bringing about a less inegalitarian America.

Of course, we can cite single cases of individual women and blacks who have succeeded in attaining high places in the professions of medicine, law, finance, journalism, and university teaching and research. However, as one author has remarked, even if there are more women in visible positions, they have not necessarily gotten there at the expense of men.[3] Overall growth (increase) in medical and law school enrollments has made possible an increase in the proportion of doctors and lawyers who are women during the 1970s; however, women have not yet begun to *replace* men at the higher income levels of these professions. In other words, society is not becoming less inegalitarian. The system has been able to absorb the rise of talented female and minority individuals. But there have been no fundamental changes in the disproportionate representation of white men in the upper ranks of power, wealth, and privilege.

Despite these discouraging aggregate statistics about American society, proponents of affirmative action can point to a number of corporate settlements in recent years in which companies have been forced to pay back wages to women and minorities, raise their salaries, and make special allowances in the future to overcome the effects of past discrimination. These settlements, starting with the $38 million settlement in 1973 in *Equal Employment Opportunity Commission* v. *American Telephone and Telegraph Company,* have been widely publicized and have involved hundreds of millions of dollars. In 1978 the General Electric Company settled an EEOC complaint by agreeing to spend $32 million on women and minority workers. That same year the Chase Manhattan Bank agreed to pay

$1.8 million to settle a suit, Uniroyal settled an EEOC suit for $5.2 million, and the *New York Times* ended a women's sex discrimination suit by agreeing to pay a $250,000 settlement and $100,000 in legal fees. In 1980 the Western Electric Company agreed to pay $7 million in back wages and other compensation to 2,200 women in two of its New Jersey plants and pledged to take a number of affirmative action steps to assure that more women were placed in better-paying jobs. Other major companies which have adopted affirmative policies to increase the number of minority and female workers in their labor force have been Inland Steel, Montgomery Ward, Sears, Roebuck, and General Motors.[4]

The American Telephone and Telegraph settlement in 1973 was a major victory for the EEOC, the National Organization for Women (NOW), and other proponents of affirmative action. American Telephone and Telegraph was the single largest private employer of women in the United States; the EEOC's final report in the case concluded that "the Bell monolith [was], without doubt, the largest oppressor of women workers in the U.S."[5] In going after "Ma Bell," the EEOC more or less accepted the arguments made by NOW representatives concerning the existence of institutionalized sex discrimination and sex stereotyping throughout the entire Bell system. The statistics supplied by American Telephone and Telegraph on the composition of its labor force merely confirmed this picture of occupational segregation. The final settlement therefore included not only a financial award but also strong insistence that future Bell system employment practices integrate men into women's jobs as well as advance women into men's.

With this settlement, the EEOC accepted feminist arguments that any job category that remained solely female (or black) would contribute to the maintenance of sex-role and race stereotypes and, with that, the psychological aspects of discrimination. A second positive result of the case was a reorientation of the EEOC's strategy with regard to major corporations. The EEOC set up its new National Programs Division to investigate cases of national significance where there are multiple complaints. This reorientation, coupled with a broadening of the EEOC's powers in 1972—as a result of the Equal Employment Opportunity Act of 1972, the EEOC was given the right to sue in court—prepared the commission to pursue the large corporate settlements cited above. In many important ways, then, the American Telephone and Telegraph case set a precedent for later successes.

Other accomplishments to which proponents of affirmative action may point are the number of recent cases in which the federal government has applied its own regulations to its own agencies. In March, 1980, for example, the U.S. Judicial Conference[6] ordered all federal courts to adopt immediately an affirmative action plan to provide equality in job opportunities for racial minorities and women.[7] The plan, intended to cover all court personnel including staffs of judges and court officers (the federal courts employ about twelve thousand persons), was imposed as the result of a petition filed in 1979 by a coalition of civil rights groups. As for the executive branch, in January, 1981, the outgoing Carter administration settled a job discrimination suit by agreeing to replace one of the government's basic civil service examinations.[8] Members of minority groups had charged that the Professional and Administrative Career Examination (known as the PACE exam)[9] discriminated against blacks and Hispanic Americans. While the government, in its consent decree, did not acknowledge that the test was discriminatory, Justice Department lawyers said that they believed the government would have lost if the case had gone to trial.

Despite these reforms, however, the record of the federal government with respect to affirmative action is not unmixed. Members of Congress, exempt from the many laws they have passed on civil rights and equal opportunity, pay female employees lower salaries than they do male employees and give them fewer top jobs.[10] And in a somewhat unusual case filed in October, 1980, the state of New York sued the federal government, charging that it had failed to enforce its own regulations requiring federally assisted construction contractors to increase the employment opportunities of women and minority group members. The suit did not seek damages but simply asked the U.S. Department of Labor to enforce its own guidelines concerning hiring practices.[11]

To summarize, we might say that there have been some victories for affirmative action, notably in a series of major corporate settlements and in the partial determination of the federal government to put its own house in order. At the same time, the situation, in aggregate terms, of blacks and women in America has not improved over the last fifteen years. It seems that the policy of affirmative action has not resulted in a less inegalitarian society. We turn now to examine why this is the case.

Recurring difficulties in administering affirmative action constitute one major reason for the failure of this policy to alter significantly the distribution of opportunities and privileges in the United States. These difficulties include confusion and lack of clarity about what the federal guidelines required; resort to evasionary tactics by employers; structural difficulties concerning the status of those designated as affirmative action officers in corporations and universities; and failures on the part of federal agencies to vigorously enforce the guidelines. In recent years, as more ethnic groups have been included under the umbrella of affirmative action, the policy has had to face more serious challenge and criticism. Each of these points deserves some comment.

Initially, affirmative action rules and regulations were criticized as vague and unclear; public controversy in the late 1960s and 1970s about goals and quotas is evidence of the confusion that existed in the minds of employers, administrators, and the general public about what exactly was required under federal guidelines. As this controversy gradually subsided and employers began to understand the requirements, some began to develop novel, ingenious methods of noncompliance. For example, a favorite evasionary tactic has been to tailor a job description in an advertisement so narrowly and specifically that most prospective candidates are effectively prevented at the outset from applying for the position. A second form of noncompliance has been tokenism—the idea that, rather than revise personnel and hiring procedures to create genuinely equal access to all jobs, an employer could simply hire one or two blacks and/or women as "proof" of compliance with the law.

In addition to such misunderstandings of, and attempts to evade, affirmative action obligations, policy implementation in corporate and academic institutions has suffered from what might be called structural problems with respect to those designated as affirmative action officers. The typical corporate or academic affirmative action officer is usually saddled not only with affirmative action responsibilities but with five or six other projects, which means that only a limited amount of time can be devoted to affirmative action. More important, he or she is usually appointed by and responsible to the firm's president or chief executive; as a result the officer has considerable job vulnerability and is not at all in a position to ride herd on an administration which is dragging its feet on affirmative action. Obviously, in a business or academic institution no affirmative action officer can achieve much without the full, active support of the executive hierarchy or university administration.

The failure of federal agencies vigorously to enforce guidelines and regulations is yet another reason that affirmative action has not altered significantly the distributional patterns of American society. Initially the federal agencies (the Office of Civil Rights, the Department of Justice, the Equal Employment Opportunity Commission, and the Office of Federal Contract Compliance) were swamped with individual complaints. By 1974 the EEOC had more than 100,000 cases outstanding, a backlog so huge that many individuals simply gave up. Under the chairmanship of Eleanor Holmes Norton, the commission revised and streamlined its procedures and managed to reduce the backlog.

The federal enforcement effort also suffered initially from confusion among various agencies about interpretation of the law.[12] Moreover, the usual ills of bureaucracy plagued the government enforcement effort. Policy implementation was so fragmented and decentralized—sixteen different agencies had some responsibility for some part of the effort—that lax, inefficient law enforcement was perhaps inevitable. As a result, business and academic institutions faced a confusing array of agencies and bureaus, each with somewhat distinct yet overlapping requirements. In 1978 the Carter administration reorganized and centralized the antidiscrimination effort into two agencies, the EEOC and the OFCC. In these ways the federal government has responded to the criticism of lax enforcement of its equal opportunity regulations.

Perhaps the most serious difficulty in the administration of affirmative action programs in recent years has been the expansion of the number of protected groups who might qualify as recipients of preferential treatment. Although the affirmative action laws grew out of the civil rights statutes of the mid-1960s, they were eventually expanded to groups other than blacks and now include women, American Indians, Hispanic-Americans, and Asian-Americans (this last category includes all Americans of Chinese, Japanese, Korean, Aleut, and Philippine descent, and anyone with roots in "the Far East" and "subcontinent India"). In addition, the aged, the handicapped, and Vietnam veterans have qualified for special treatment under affirmative action programs. As a result of this accordion-like expansion of protected classes, a debate has developed among civil rights and affirmative action proponents. They question whether blacks are put at a disadvantage by the active competition of women and others for special assist ance or whether they are helped by the provision of new allies in their efforts to influence government and industry. This debate and the problem it reflects is most serious in the competition between the two protected classes which are best organized—white women and blacks of both sexes. Needless to say, the problem is exacerbated by recession, inflation, and high unemployment.

In 1979 a remarkable lawsuit *(Sears, Roebuck and Company* v. *Attorney General of the United States, et al)* was filed, which dramatically illustrated this problem. Sears, Roebuck and Company, the largest retailer in the United States, filed suit against ten federal agencies, saying that it could not follow their directives on equal employment opportunity.[13] Sears charged that government laws, regulations, interpretations, and policies were so confusing, conflicting, and inconsistent that they could not be complied with. In particular, the Sears lawsuit traced the history of affirmative action to World War II and to policies giving military veterans preference as they returned to civilian society. Since the military at that time was dominated by white males, the company argued, Sears, by complying with the laws of the times, left itself in a difficult position to catch up with the changing laws and attitudes of the 1960s, which emphasized preference for minorities and women. The Sears lawsuit also contended that a 1978 congressional amendment to the Age Discrimination in Employment Act, which extended the time of retirement from sixty-five to seventy years of age, had further complicated efforts to hire and promote minorities and women.

The Sears complaint asked that the government be prohibited from enforcing antidiscrimination measures against the company until it clarified its priorities and procedures. Sears requested, among other things, "an injunction requiring the defendants to coordinate the enforcement of the antidiscrimination statutes and, specifically, to issue uniform guidelines which instruct employers how to resolve existing conflicts between affirmative action requirements based on race and sex and those based on veterans' status, age and physical or mental handicaps."[14]

The disposition of this case was not favorable to Sears, Roebuck and Company. On May 15, 1979, Judge June L. Green of the federal district court in Washington dismissed the suit on grounds that the Sears complaint was insufficiently concrete to give the company standing to sue. In declaring that the Sears case was more hypothetical than real, Judge Green cited the "case and controversy" rule of Article III of the U.S. Constitution, which limits the power of the Federal judiciary to the adjudication of actual, real legal disputes. "A concrete factual setting and an adverse legal relationship, which the judicial power is capable of resolving, are essential requirements," Judge Green declared.[15]

In dismissing the case on procedural grounds, Judge Green recognized that, since 1973, the EEOC had been investigating allegations of job discrimination at Sears but had not yet filed charges against the company. The judge's decision implied that Sears could not raise the issues it listed in its complaint until actual, specific charges had been brought against the company by the federal government. Once suit was filed and an actual legal dispute was underway, then Sears could raise its contentions about veterans' preference in answering charges brought against it by the EEOC.

The Sears lawsuit must be seen in the context of the company's own difficulties with the EEOC.[16] While Sears had insisted that its suit was serious litigation, the view in some legal circles was that the company had gone to court primarily for public relations reasons. In this view, Sears sought to win sympathy for itself before the government filed charges against it.[17]

Although this ingenious lawsuit was dismissed, it nevertheless dramatized the problem of pursuing affirmative action under conditions of scarcity. When the majority of Americans are covered by protective statutes, who gets jobs when not all can? What about the expansion of protected classes under affirmative action? Are there now so many protected groups that none are protected? Specifically, are blacks, the originally intended beneficiaries of affirmative action, losing out to other groups?

There are some who insist that the true beneficiaries of affirmative action have been white women. And indeed we have documented, in the preceding chapters, how the addition of sex discrimination to Title VII of the 1964 Civil Rights Act and the expansion of the executive orders concerning affirmative action to include sex as well as racial discrimination provided legal tools which were used actively and aggressively by women to improve their employment possibilities. Yet, as the aggregate statistics cited at the beginning of this chapter show, neither blacks as a group nor women as a group have benefited from affirmative action. Single minority and female individuals may have improved their job possibilities and life chances, but the overall distributional pattern of American society has not changed measurably. Moreover, given economic retrenchment, minorities and women may lose what few gains they have made.[18]

It would be foolish to ignore the problem of competition among protected classes in times of economic scarcity. At the same time, racism and sexism are twin evils, related manifestations of an underlying injustice—arbitrary discrimination by a society still arranged so as to give undue preference to white males who own capital. Until systemic structural changes occur, the evils of racism and sexism will not be eliminated. In the absence of basic structural reform, the expansion in accordion-like fashion of the number of protected groups who may benefit from affirmative action must be greeted with a certain amount of skepticism. Such accordion-like expansion seems reminiscent of a divide-and-conquer approach on the part of established groups in society. For such elites, an alternative to equitable redistribution of ownership and control of capital is to adopt policies which set minorities and women fighting amongst themselves for a few limited opportunities. As one affirmative action officer put it: "If we argue about who comes first, then the man has us fighting among ourselves. This is divisiveness in the extreme."[19]

The fundamental antidote to such harmful competition among the beneficiaries of affirmative action is to forge alliances among the competing groups and to press in united fashion, as a coalition, for necessary changes in the proprietary (capitalist) character of business, industry, and the professions.

Thus far we have discussed some of the recurring difficulties in implementing affirmative action policies. Confusion about policy requirements, evasionary tactics, and lack of vigorous enforcement by federal agencies usually affect implementation of any public policy. But this last problem concerning the expansion of groups which are to benefit from affirmative action points to deeper reasons why affirmative action has not succeeded in reducing inequalities in American society.

Affirmative action is a single policy effort, unsupported by other social policies designed to realize greater equality. In a sense, it is a lonely policy, a voice in the wilderness. Without the support of other policies directed at reducing disparities in wealth, status, and power in American society, little can be achieved.

Secondly, affirmative action is a policy which may be appropriate in times of economic expansion but which probably cannot achieve much in recessionary times. The Sears lawsuit (described above) and the competition among potential beneficiaries of affirmative action testify to the problematic character and the limited effectiveness of this policy.

Thirdly, insofar as affirmative action departs from strict and sole reliance upon the merit principle as the criterion for assigning positions and places in society, affirmative action may be characterized as a radical policy. Yet, its potentially radical thrust is blunted and thwarted by its essentially conservative character. For affirmative action is designed to conserve liberal-capitalism, not to change it. It coopts talented women and minorities into the ranks of the business and professional elites without challenging fundamental class inequalities and inequities in American society. It introduces some members of hitherto disadvantaged groups into the mainstream of the American economy without changing the basic way in which that economy functions. In this sense affirmative action is a method of cooptation, a typically liberal, reformist response to patterns of systemic injustice which call for radical change.

Admittedly, this conclusion could be contested. After all, many women and minorities (not merely a few professionals) have benefited from settlements such as the American Telephone and Telegraph agreement or the Philadelphia Plan. And all women and minorities stand to gain from the breakdown of stereotypic thinking which has occurred in the last fifteen years. Yet, the aggregate statistics cited at the beginning of this chapter tell the real story about the achievements of affirmative action. While basic attitudinal changes are important, they must be accompanied by concrete achievements in occupational desegregation and in reduction of the earnings gap between the races and the sexes if we are to judge affirmative action a success.

This does not mean that the policy of affirmative action is to be judged a total failure and be abandoned forthwith. Rather, we must adjust our expectations and be more realistic about what affirmative action can and cannot do. We must acknowledge that affirmative action *of itself* cannot achieve much in solving the problem of unjust disparities in power and privilege among different groups in American society. It must be recognized that this problem is a systemic one requiring fundamental changes in our capitalist political economy.

If we ask what it is that affirmative action affirms about American society, we can say that it affirms a commitment to greater equality. But it also illustrates and affirms the complexity of social problems. Finally, it affirms the poverty of

American welfare-state liberalism. Affirmative action illustrates the limitations of state and institutional attempts to create equality in a society where inequalities are mainly the result of structural characteristics inhering in a capitalist economy.

The controversy over affirmative action during the last fifteen years may have diverted and distracted Americans from the fundamental structural changes which are necessary if American society is to become less inegalitarian. In chapters 8 and 9 below, we seek to rethink the notion of equality and to examine the kinds of fundamental changes which are necessary.

SECTION THREE

Where Should We Go from Here?

8

Thinking Clearly about Equality: Conceptual Premises and Why They Make a Difference

Bette Novit Evans

> The terms of political discourse set the frame within which political thought and action proceed. To examine that discourse is to translate tacit judgments embedded in the language of politics into explicit considerations more fully subject to critical assessment.
>
> **William Connolly**
> *The Terms of Political Discourse*

At first glance, making an argument in favor of equality today seems to offer all the excitement of getting into a fight after it has been won. Almost no one makes serious claims in favor of *in*equality these days. No serious thinker, for example, still maintains that certain classes of people are inherently inferior to other classes, and even those who may still think so have the good sense not to admit it publicly. Social policies conducive to greater equality may not be fashionable in America these days, but equality as a goal is widely considered valid (if not necessarily viable). Why, then, continue the argument?

Part of the answer lies in the fact that even when we agree on equality as a principle, we may disagree radically on what that principle implies. Both proponents and opponents of compensatory programs rest their cases on conceptions of equality, differently understood. Policies involving rewards or incentives run headlong into the issue of equality. Attempts to promote justice, whether in the legal system or in the distribution of goods and services, force one to confront the issue of equality. Contemporary political controversy is replete with issues which lead us to consider questions about equality. Behind these issues are the classical concerns of political philosophy: justice, obligation, authority, community. Premises about human equality and inequality underlie arguments we make on all these subjects. In fact, we are convinced that moral philosophy in general, insofar as it attempts to formulate principles that are universalizable, rests on premises regarding the equality of human beings as moral agents. Wherever we look, equality seems to underlie many of our concerns and debates.

In fact, our disagreements often fall short of being arguments at all. Disagreements on basic assumptions, often unstated, leave us without common ground from which to approach the subject and hence without agreement on legitimate ways of asking the appropriate questions. The problem is not that we disagree on the substantive issues, but rather that our premises and our logic are not clear enough to allow us to argue intelligently at all. What is needed, therefore, is some clearheaded thinking about philosophical premises, so that we can at least know where we stand and how our starting points will affect the directions our arguments take. The purpose of this chapter is to render explicit some of the underlying issues of the major arguments about equality—both in the literature of political theory and in contemporary public policy controversies.

In the second section we consider what it means to assert that people are equal or unequal as a matter of fact; we want to understand the meaning and the logic of these factual assertions in order to examine their implications for public policy. The third section considers the ethical and metaethical issues involved in the decision that equality is something to be valued. In the fourth section we consider the practical consequences of the ambiguity of the concept of equality for political and social decisions. It is not the goal of this chapter to argue the substantive issues associated with equality, but rather to clear away some of the conceptual underbrush so that the discourse can proceed intelligently. Ultimately this chapter is based on the assumption that if we can discourse intelligently, we can improve our chances for intelligent public choice.

The assertion that people should be treated equally is frequently derived from some claim that people are in some sense equal in fact. There is a certain appeal to this kind of reasoning, but the appeal is surely not to our logical sensibilities, considering that we have known for some centuries that one cannot logically derive a normative conclusion from an empirical premise.[1] A statement that people *are* equal in fact is logically unrelated to a statement that people *should* be treated equally; they could both be accepted or rejected independently, or either one accepted and the other rejected. Still, logical niceties aside, the appeal of this assertion is too important to be so easily dismissed. What is needed to hold the argument together is a logical connective, something like the following form:

All human beings are equal.

Justice demands that equals be treated equally.

Therefore, justice demands that all human beings be treated equally.

We now have a beginning, but not a very interesting one. One reason the syllogism above sounds so uninteresting is that it strikes us as empty. Equality is an ambiguous concept. John Wilson, for example, makes a distinction between what he calls natural equality and status equality—roughly between things which are equal in the descriptive sense of the way things are (two lines are of equal length) and things which are treated equally according to human rules. Natural equality need not imply status equality and, conversely, things may be accorded equal status under any arbitrary system of rules whether they have any natural similarities or not. In our syllogism, however, the assertion was made that beings which are naturally equal should be accorded equal status.[2]

The assertion that all human beings are equal is an ambiguous one. It is not at all clear whether the assertion is intended to be an empirical statement or an analytic one. If it is an empirical claim, we have the right to demand evidence, and that will lead rather quickly to a dead end. Factual assertions about equality are not susceptible to empirical validation or falsification; hence, it seems doubtful whether factual equality could ever be satisfactorily established.

If we set out to prove that persons are equal in some empirical sense, we run into the problems that there is no evidence, no "natural fact" waiting "out there" for us to discover. Nature does not tell us what is to count as equality. Things are only equal or unequal with respect to some criterion and some measure. These do not exist in nature; they are human creations. And since we choose our criteria and measures, we cannot help embedding our findings into them.[3] In sum, equality is a human creation.

Equality involves sameness with respect to some specified attribute. Human beings are alike and are different in innumerable respects, any one of which could be selected as the one relevant to establishing equality. If we assert that people are equal, we must specify in what respects they are equal. The possibilities here are infinite. Human beings are equally bilateral, have approximately the same blood chemistry, perform approximately the same physiological functions, share the same basic genetic structure, and so forth. The problem is to specify which of these "equal" attributes is normatively relevant and to defend the choice. If I argue that the normatively relevant human attribute is blood chemistry, and you maintain that it is hair color, we have not much further to say to one another.

Furthermore, we have no agreed-upon way of specifying when differences constitute inequalities. A difference is only a difference until some normative judgment is placed upon it. A century ago black skin was not only different from white skin; it was also inferior. Today white skin and black skin are recognized as different but not unequal, except in the amount of melanin contained in the epidermal cells. In some quarters today people still argue whether anatomical differences in genital structure constitute mere differences or inequalities. It is still accepted that differences in central nervous system function or in muscular coordination can be ranked on qualitative scales: smart is not just different from stupid; it is also better. In a different culture that "fact" might come into question. As we shall see later, this ambiguity has its parallels in our evaluation of social institutions. We do not usually consider differences of treatment as inequalities unless we are going to condemn them as unjustified.

The point to be made is that if we disagree on any of these matters we cannot rely on observation to help us out of the disagreement. The issue is no longer an empirical one, but an analytical one. Therefore, it may be simpler to avoid empirical assertions altogether and to rest one's case on an analytic one: human beings are declared to be equal by definition. In effect, we would be saying that those characteristics which we define as essential to the concept of "human" are characteristics shared equally by all human beings. This, of course, is a tautology, as all definitions are. It does not give us any new information, but it does give us a place to start. This kind of statement is the same as Jefferson's famous line in the Declaration of Independence that it is "self-evident" that "all men are created equal." Utilitarians premise equality on the fact that all human beings are capable of suffering and of experiencing pleasure; liberals see the capacity for reason as the essential shared human attribute. Existentialists argue that the fact of existence makes people equal and that all are equal in their responsibility for their own choices. Such arguments are premised on the existence of some shared human capacity. This is an appealing premise, but one which is not open to verification or falsification. A capacity is only a potentiality, which may or may not be manifested or realized. The discovery of a person who demonstrates no ability to reason, for example, is inconclusive regarding the issue of whether or not that person has the capacity to reason. In short, it is impossible to demonstrate whether or not such a capacity exists.

Given the numerous and obvious differences among people, egalitarians must distinguish between differences that are significant and those which are not. When we define people as equal "in essence" or "in nature," we are making an implicit distinction between what is essential and what is accidental, between what one *is* and what one *has*. In Wilson's words:

> The question of whether one game or system gives a person more equality of opportunity than another game or system depends ultimately on what we count as a person. The egalitarian adopts a narrow picture, whereby a person *is* determined and courageous, but only *has* intelligence, wealth, and a title. But this picture is not compulsory; we might alternatively say that a person *is* determined, courageous, intelligent, rich, and aristocratic. Or we could outdo the egalitarian and say that he *has* determination and courage rather than that he *is* determined and courageous. So far as logic and language go, it seems arbitrary which picture we choose to adopt.[4]

The egalitarian must try to account for observed inequalities as accidental, epiphenomenal, nonessential, rather than natural and necessary. No one labored more seriously to present such an argument than Rousseau in his *Discourse on the Origin of Inequality,* and no one has become more entangled in tortured reasoning in trying to distinguish "nature" from "society." Rousseau argued that all persons are equal in the state of nature and that inequalities are the products of society. But since society is created by "natural" persons, without unnatural intervention, it is hard to accept Rosseau's conclusion that social inequalities are somehow "unnatural."[5]

Closely akin to the issue of natural and nonnatural equalities is the issue of the inevitability of inequalities. We do not condemn a practice as unjust if we are convinced it could not be otherwise. It is only those inequalities which we believe could be remedied which become the subject of ethical discourse. Not only linguistically but psychologically, "ought" implies "can." However, we disagree profoundly over what can or cannot be changed.

John Rawls, in *A Theory of Justice,* makes clear that the distribution of natural abilities is not itself subject to ethical evaluation. Natural inequalities are neither just nor unjust; they are simply natural facts: "The natural distribution is neither just nor unjust; nor it is unjust that persons are born into society at some particular position. These are simply natural facts. What is just and unjust is the way that institutions deal with these facts."[6]

Rawls may be correct that we need not consider the justice of natural differences, but the inevitability of such inequalities should not be a foregone conclusion. What seems inevitable in one era seems easily remediable in another. For most of human history, basic inequalities of mental and physical endowments were considered to be unalterable facts of nature. In this century we have discovered to what extent these capabilities are environmentally determined. We now know that nutrition, health care, and child-rearing practices substantially affect one's mental and physical capabilities. Having acquired the ability, through environmental engineering, to equalize these factors (improving those which are deficient), we would probably consider it unjust to fail to do so. Shall we not some day make the same argument about genetic inequalities? Hereditary deficiencies no longer seem as unalterable as they once did. Increasingly, people support genetic counseling, prenatal testing, and research into gene repair. In the future it may not seem any more unnatural to try to equalize genetic endowments than it now does to equalize environmental influences on basic capabilities.

Economic, social, and political inequalities, although human contrivances, may be more nearly inevitable than the previously considered natural ones. It is possible to imagine a system of absolute economic equality (monastic communities, Spartan-like military organizations, and utopian communities come to mind), but it seems clear that such equality could be achieved only with the radical sacrifice of other values.

Whether social and political equality are possible at all is the subject of considerable disagreement. John Plamenatz points out that as long as there is any division of labor in any society—even division of sexual function, or division based on age—there is inequality. As long as there is social approbation for outstanding achievements, or such values as honor and excellence, there necessarily is inequality. In short, the concept of organized society implies inequality.[7] All but the most radical egalitarians admit this limitation, but they argue that it is possible to limit and to rationalize social inequalities.[8]

Political inequality is the subject of considerable dispute. Enlightenment radicals such as Tom Paine believed that absolute political equality could be possible; the Athenian system of universal citizen participation and officeholding by lot served as their model. Nineteenth-century socialists and anarchists continued this tradition. Contemporary political science, for the most part, rejects this premise and argues that the very concept of politics implies the existence of inequality. By definition, power signifies an asymmetrical relationship. Any concept of rule, government, bureaucracy, or related term implies that some people are empowered to make decisions and others are not. Max Weber pioneered this conventional understanding of power.[9] Robert Dahl exemplifies this notion when he directs our attention away from the search for political equality and toward the distinction between cumulative and dispersed inequalities.[10] It should be pointed out that not all political thinkers accept Dahl's characterization, and a lively debate continues over the possibility of equalizing political participation.[11]

We have been exploring these disputes over the inevitability of inequalities in an effort to understand factual assertions regarding equality. When the egalitarian defines people as equal by virtue of some shared human capacity, he must confront evidence that people seem to exercise these capacities to varying degrees. We cannot help noticing that some people seem to have better reasoning capacity than others; some seem better able to make moral choices; some even seem more conscious of their humanity than others. In light of this difficulty, the egalitarian may want to avoid any assertion of equality of any characteristic that is quantifiable, even in the ordinal sense. Some characteristics do not lend themselves to comparison at all. All people have interests. All people have intentions. All people have needs. (So, unfortunately, do dogs and dolphins, and some day we may discover that roses and cabbages do as well. But no matter.) It simply does not make sense to say that John can intend more than Jim, or that Jane has more interests than Joan. [12]

The apparently academic issue of the nonquantifiable character by which we may define human equality has considerable import in our public policy choices. Equality based on shared rational capacity quite clearly excludes those people to whom we do not impute rationality, such as those who are mentally retarded. If we see rationality as the defining characteristic for human existence, we are likely to think that mentally retarded persons deserve less consideration than others because they fall below our defining parameter of "equal" human beings. But if the defining parameter is having interests (or needs, or desires, which are not at all the same), then it is clear that mentally deficient people have interests, needs, or desires equally with everyone else. (Note that the foregoing statement indicates that they equally *have* interests, not that they have *equal* interests. The grammatical difference indicates the point of noncomparability.) Under such a notion, we are much more likely to believe that such persons have an equal right to have their interests or needs considered, and thus to favor education and legal rights for the mentally retarded.

The egalitarian tendencies of socialist theories can be explained by the reliance on a nonquantifiable conception of what is basic to humanity. Socialists tend to define the normatively relevant human attributes as needs. Since human beings equally have needs, socialists are led to argue for equal consideration in the statisfaction of these needs.

Contemporary thinkers tend to rely on these kinds of nonquantifiable statements in making arguments about equality. The problem with such statements, and with analytic statements in general, is that they will not convince anyone. They are simply matters of definition. A definition is there to be accepted or rejected, and if it is rejected the discourse ends there.

One may be tempted, therefore, not to worry about the definitions and premises. Nevertheless, both the egalitarian and his adversaries ought to be concerned about them because premises and definitions profoundly influence the sorts of policy choices we make. Some definitions of equality lead more readily to demands for equal social and material conditions than do others. In any case, between the factual assertion and the policy choice there always lies an intervening step: the ethical assertion. Even if we agree that human beings are equal in some relevant respect, we cannot automatically conclude that they must be treated equally in any other respect. Such a conclusion involves us in an ethical argument.

The claim that people should be treated equally is an ethical claim, and to pursue it involves us in ethical discourse. Such a claim requires justification. One may legitimately ask, "Why should I treat people equally?" One quite proper response may be, "Why not?" The answer is not at all facetious but is a statement about presumption and burden of proof. If presumption lies on the side of equality, then any inequality needs special justification. On the other hand, if one is required from the outset to build and defend a prima facie case for equality, the task is much more difficult.

There is an analogous issue in current American legal controversy regarding equality and discrimination. Are we to presume that people are being treated equally unless discrimination is proven, or may we infer discrimination from certain patterns of inequalities and presume it to be the case unless the opposite is proven? Recent U.S. Supreme Court decisions on de facto school segregation (e.g., *Keyes* v. *Denver School District No. 1*) illustrate the importance of this point. If schools are racially unbalanced, can discrimination be presumed to have occurred, or must the intent to discriminate be proven before remedial measures are required? Similar issues of burden of proof arise in the legal campaign for equal housing, employment, and administration of justice. The attempt by feminists to have gender declared a suspect category is also a matter of burden of proof. Without such a declaration, sexual classifications are taken at face value unless discriminatory intent is established. If sexual classifications are ever declared suspect, any such classification will be assumed discriminatory unless the opposite can be proved.

If I claim to value equality, you may legitimately ask me why it is of value. I may answer that equality is right or good in itself. Or, I may argue that equality is necessary for the attainment of some other value. Stated more succinctly, equality may be considered a deontological value, or an instrumental one. If I hold equality to be a deontological value, I may do so by noting that equality is implicit in the concept of justice and of morality itself.

Much of our confusion about the value of equality, as we have said, lies in the fact that the word "equal" is a normatively ambiguous word. "Two lines of equal length" is simply a descriptive phrase. "The two children were not treated equally," however, is not only a description, but a complaint that one child has been treated unjustly. Assuming, for the sake of argument, that we hold justice to be a deontological value, our question is whether or not equality is definitionally related to justice.

Hugo A. Bedau argues rather convincingly that equality is not definitionally related to justice. Certainly, a distribution can be just without being equal and can be equal without being just.[13] If a judge sends an innocent man and a criminal both to jail, he may be treating them equally, but he certainly would not be treating the innocent man justly. Conversely, if a professor in assigning grades gives an *A* to an excellent paper and a *C* to a mediocre one he has not given them equal grades, but he may be grading them justly.

And yet, there is more to be said to complicate matters. No matter what definition of justice we use, we run into the notion that justice has something to do with treating like cases alike.[14] If two defendants committed the same crime, with similar motivations, under similar circumstances, we would feel that justice had not been done if one received a heavy penalty and the other were set free. That is to say, the concept of justice is intimately bound up with the idea of treating equals equally. Indeed, any concept of a rule or principle implies treating equal cases alike.[15]

This notion can be extended back to the concept of interpersonal morality itself. One attribute of a moral rule is that it is one we would be willing to universalize, to apply, or see applied, in every case of the same nature. Whenever we talk about universalizable rules, we find ourselves talking about treating like cases alike. The concept of justice, then, is implicit in this concept of interpersonal morality. And within both concepts there lies the principle of equality. Through this circuitous route, then, we may arrive at the position that any concept of morality based on universalizability implies the value of equality. Equality, then, is moral and just because it is an important element of the very concept of morality and justice. So conceived, we arrive at the point where we may argue that equality is to be valued as a deontological good.

If one rejects the foregoing argument, that person may wish to maintain that equality is to be valued because it is instrumental for the attainment of some other good. One who argues that equality is an instrumental value faces a complex task. He must be prepared to specify the value for which equality is instrumental and to bring evidence (and refute counterevidence) to show that equality will facilitate the achievement of this value. I might, for example, argue that political equality is necessary to achieve social cohesion, or that it provides the best likelihood of producing good public policy. I might argue that equality of economic opportunity is instrumental in achieving the most efficient production and distribution of wealth, or that racial equality is necessary for maintaining social harmony, or that sexual equality is necessary for efficient utilization of labor power.

Even if we overcome these difficulties and agree that equality is to be valued, we still must decide how equality is to be ranked among other values. Is equality to be preeminent among values, or is it to be one of a number of competing values to be traded off against each other, without reference to a fixed hierarchy? In making public policy, just how important is our concern for equality? If equality is to be considered nonnegotiable and preeminent, then we must be prepared to accept the subordination of other values. For example, both socialist and capitalist economists agree that, in any economic system, there is a threshold beyond which increasing economic equality produces economic inefficiency, thereby tending to impoverish everyone.[16] Economists disagree, however, over the point at which the values of equality and efficiency come into conflict, and which should be sacrificed. Within the liberal tradition, as we have seen, there is a strong conviction that the pursuit of equality conflicts with the values of liberty and individualism. In the conservative tradition, equality is seen as conflicting with the values of excellence in aesthetic, spiritual, or intellectual pursuits.

Bedau suggests that if we consider equality as merely instrumental, as conceptually distinct from justice, then it is rather easy to justify sacrificing equality for some more pressing value.[17] The principle, "Treat people equally unless there is good reason to treat them differently," leaves ample opportunity for one to discover "good reasons" for disregarding equality. Utilitarians begin with the most egalitarian of principles, but because aggregate pleasure is the only final ethical principle, it is easy for utilitarians to justify the most inegalitarian institutions when doing so maximizes goods for the greatest number.[18]

Let us consider an example from the forefront of current civil rights controversies in the United States: the controversy over the rights of the mentally handicapped to equal public education. If equality of treatment is a nonnegotiable value, then one might say that it is only right to provide equal educational facilities for the retarded. If, on the other hand, one considers equal educational facilities as only one of the legitimate values for which the commonwealth must allocate its scarce resources, then one has to weigh the benefits and the costs of that policy against the benefits and costs of alternative expenditures (graduate education for the brightest students, medical research to prevent retardation, military equipment and personnel). In every case, the relative position of the value determines the outcome of the policy decision.

Having suggested some of the issues raised in ethical discourse about equality, let us now consider the implications of these ethical issues for the making of public policy. Let us even assume that we have agreed that equality is to be valued, and we are striving with good intentions to design public policy to treat people equally. As we shall see, the ethical ambiguity of the concept of equality has its parallel in the realm of political choice.

The political activist may be understandably annoyed with the foregoing discussion. Endless disputations on the meaning of meaning can mask an abdication of one's responsibility to choose and to act. Without disregarding this danger, we are arguing here that principled choice *relies* on clear understanding of principle. Thus, if we hold equality to be a political value, we must be clear about what it means to treat people equally. Equality is a highly ambiguous word, and this ambiguity leads people who agree on the principle to act in utterly opposite ways.

People and situations have countless attributes; treating them equally with respect to one attribute often means treating them unequally with respect to others. Educators are painfully familiar with this problem as it impinges on the assignment of grades. An instructor may receive two equally good student papers, one produced by an average but meticulous student after considerable effort, the other thrown together off the top of the head by a very bright student, or one with a good background in the subject, with little effort at all. If the instructor judges then by equal standards on the basis of product, he is disregarding the clear inequality of effort. If he grades them on the basis of the unequal effort, on the other hand, he is forced to disregard the equality of the product. Even the instructor with the best intentions of grading on equal standards finds himself perplexed at how to do so.

The same problem appears in the recurring questions associated with labor compensation. Liberal economists are adamant on the principle of equality, but equality applies to the equal opportunity to enjoy the fruits of one's labor. To provide the enjoyment of goods disproportionate to the contribution of labor, strikes the traditional liberal as a gross inequality and an injustice. Marx finds himself in the same position when he criticizes the simplistically egalitarian proposals of the Social Democratic Gotha Program. In the early stages of communism, Marx explains, socialist equality will not be very different from the ideal expressed (but rarely effected) by the liberals:

> The individual producer receives back from society—after the deductions have been made—exactly what he gives to it. What he has given to it is his individual quantum of labor. . . . The same amount of labor which he has given to society in one form he receives back in another. . . . The right of the producers is *proportional* to the labor they supply; the equality consists in the fact that measurement is made with an *equal standard,* labor. But one man is superior to another physically or mentally, and so supplies more labor in the same time, or can labor for a longer time; and labor, to serve as a measure, must be defined by its duration or intensity; otherwise, it ceases to be a standard of measurement. This *equal* right is an unequal right for unequal labor. It recognizes no class differences because everyone is only a worker like everyone else, but it tacitly recognizes unequal individual endowment and thus productive capacity as natural privileges. *It is, therefore, a right of inequality, in its content, like every right.* Right by its very nature can consist only in the application of an equal standard, but unequal individuals (and they would not be different individuals if they were not unequal) are measurable only by an equal standard in so far as they are brought under an equal point of view, are taken from one *definite* side only, for instance, in the present case, are regarded *only as workers,* and, nothing more is seen in them, everything else being ignored. Further, one worker is married, another not; one has more children than another, and so on and so forth. Thus, with an equal performance of labor, and hence an equal share in the social consumption fund, one will in fact receive more than another, one will be richer than another, and so on. To avoid all these defects, right instead of being equal would have to be unequal.[19]

We may agree that in employment opportunities people should be treated equally, but disagree vehemently on whether equality demands or forbids affirmative action. A policy of preferential hiring for minorities is defended, as we have seen, in terms of equalizing a system that has awarded unearned advantages based upon irrelevant attributes. It also may be attacked as providing unearned advantages based on irrelevant attributes. To settle the matter, we would have to return to our earlier question of distinguishing the relevant from the irrelevant attributes of human beings. Until we do so, the concept of equality remains uselessly ambiguous.

It is impossible to determine whether we are treating people alike or differently until we can agree on the variable or attribute that is relevant. This difficulty becomes clear in an example adapted from one used by Bedau. A parent with two children wants to treat them equally in buying them musical instruments. One child wants a guitar; the other wants a piano. If the parent buys each child what he wants, he may be accused of spending considerably more on one child than on the other. On the other hand, if he buys pianos for both, he may be accused of treating them unequally by buying one what he wants and the other what he does not want.[20]

This problem is magnified when we have to decide whether to give equal consideration to people's interests or to their wants. If I plan to enroll my two children in music lessons, and one wants to take piano lessons, and the other wants to learn to play the police whistle, I would probably feel justified in telling the second child that equal consideration of his interests demands my giving unequal consideration to his wants. (For the loyal devotees of police whistles, imagine that in ordering lunch, one child chooses a vegetable platter and the other orders six candy bars). Here, the well-intentioned egalitarian is faced with a legitimate dilemma. If he takes account of wants or desires and tries to give equal consideration to everyone's wants, he finds himself in an absurd position: some wants are simply illegitimate, harmful, and deserving of no serious consideration. The rapist's desire to rape should not be considered equal to the victim's desire not to be raped. Some people's desires may count for less than those of others: the convict's desire for freedom is not taken into account, not because of the content of the desire, but because of the status of the person. On the other hand, if the well-meaning egalitarian decides that he need not consider all wants as equal, but must equally consider everyone's true interests, then he must allocate to someone the authority to decide what is everyone's "true" interest, and soon there is not much left of the principle of equality.[21]

Given the multitudes of differences among people, it is abundantly clear that treating people the same does not imply treating them equally. Treating the rich and the poor alike in the criminal justice process sounds like a good idea until one considers the costs of legal counsel and court documents, time spent away from employment or the chance of employment, and costs attendant upon returning to society after incarceration. In this light, we discover that equal justice may require treating rich and poor differently—for example, providing free legal assistance to indigents (as in *Gideon* v. *Wainwright*). All our programs of assistance to disadvantaged persons can be seen as attempts to equalize conditions and, simultaneously, as programs which treat people unequally.

This problem returns to our attention the question of distinguishing between differences and inequalities. Not even the strictest egalitarian would demand that everyone be treated alike—that we treat a sick person like a healthy one or an aged person like a young one. Any system of role differentiation implies that people have different functions, activities, responsibilities, and the like. Ordinarily we do not call these differences inequalities unless we are complaining that a difference operates to unfairly disadvantage someone.[22] We do not complain, for example, of unequal rights because judges are permitted to send people to jail, and carpenters are not permitted to do so. Until recently, no one would have thought to attack as unequal laws which exempt women from compulsory military obligation. *A difference may be natural; a difference that disadvantages someone on grounds that we consider irrelevant and discriminatory is one which we call an inequality.* Therefore, in any movement to achieve a new equality, the first and most crucial step is convincing people that the kind of treatment which was previously considered only different is not only different but also unequal. The classic example in American history is the separate-but-equal doctrine established in *Plessy* v. *Ferguson*. When a law requiring separate but equal railway cars for blacks and whites was originally upheld by the Supreme Court, the Court expressed the view that separate facilities were differences which were, normatively speaking, strictly neutral. The difference did not constitute an inequality in

1896. In Justice Brown's words:

> We consider the underlying fallacy of the plaintiff's argument to consist in the assumption that the enforced separation of the two races stamps the colored race with a badge of inferiority. If this is so, it is not by reason of anything found in the act, but solely because the colored race chooses to put that construction upon it.

The importance of the *Brown* v. *Board of Education* decision fifty-eight years later was that the Court now embraced the notion that separate facilities were not merely a difference in treatment, but were a difference that constituted, on its face, an inequality. Chief Justice Warren's words are explicit:

> To separate [children in grade and high schools] from others of similar age and qualifications solely because of their race generates a feeling of inferiority as to their status in the community that may affect their hearts and minds in a way unlikely ever to be undone.... We conclude that in the field of public education the doctrine of "separate but equal" has no place. Separate educational facilities are inherently unequal.

In our era the most difficult task of the women's rights movement has been to convince people (many women included) that different role expectations are not only neutrally different but are unequal in the normative sense.

Finally, the issue of equality is complicated by an ambiguity over *what* should be treated equally. What is the proper unit of analysis? If we value equality as an attribute of the society as an aggregate, we may have to sacrifice equality individually in the treatment of particular cases. Progressive taxation, social insurance, welfare programs, and compensatory programs all strive (theoretically) to equalize conditions within the aggregate by dealing with individuals unequally. For example, progressive taxation policies treat people differently in order to redistribute wealth. We tax people progressively, i.e., at different rates in order to equalize economic inequalities within the commonwealth.

The distinction between aggregate and individual equality is easily apparent in the rhetoric of international relations. We frequently hear demands that sovereign nations be treated equally, that nations should have equal rights to self-determination without outside interference. The demand for equality of aggregate units (independent states) is not convincing to those who reject the particular aggregate as the relevant unit of analysis. If a state which denies equality to individuals within its borders then demands equal treatment among nations, citing the principle of equality, this demand appears as a disingenuous shifting of ground. The human rights controversy in international diplomacy, current during the Carter administration, can be seen as a dispute over the proper unit on which to rest demands for equality.

Even within the United States there has been a long and bitter history of controversy over this matter of aggregates or individuals. The early debate over whether the United States was a confederation of states or a union of persons and the subsequent battle over dual federalism were contests of this sort. Those who demanded equality for states (equal representation in the Senate, and a states rights interpretation of the Tenth Amendment, for example) saw the state as the relevant unit to which the principle of equality must be applied. Those who stressed equal representation of individuals pointed out that policies preferred by a majority of states were often opposed by a majority of persons. Thus states rights in the twentieth century became a way of denying majority rule on such issues as economic regulation, labor legislation, various social policies, and civil rights. The larger issue of the proper unit of analysis remains unsettled, but for voting rights the individual notion was firmly and emphatically affirmed in the reapportionment cases. As Chief Justice Warren cryptically put it in *Reynolds* v. *Sims,* "Legislators represent people, not trees or acres. Legislators are elected by voters, not farms or cities or economic interests.... Citizens, not history or economic interests, cast votes."

The contemporary controversy over preferential treatment of minorities brings to the fore the political significance of the dispute over relevant units. The argument in favor of compensatory programs holds that since women and members of minority groups have been unjustly deprived of opportunities and benefits in the past, they now deserve special compensation for these losses— hence, preferential hiring and admissions programs. As we saw in chapter 6, critics contend, among other things, that it is only individuals who have been wronged and hence only individuals who deserve compensation. It is illogical, they say, to compensate one individual for the wrong done to another individual simply because they both belong to the same group. According a person special consideration because he or she is a member of a group, some of whose members have been wronged previously, is criticized as shifting illogically levels of analysis, as well as reifying the concept of the group. Consider the argument summarized by George Sher:

If the point of reverse discrimination is to compensate a wronged *group,* it will presumably hardly matter if those who are preferentially hired were not among the original victims of discrimination. However, the argument's basic presupposition, that groups as opposed to their individual members are the sorts of entities that can be wronged, and deserve redress, is itself problematic. Thus the defense of reverse discrimination would only be convincing if it were backed by a further argument showing that groups can indeed be wronged and have deserts of the relevant sort.[23]

Behind this point lies the problem that two different kinds of equality are in conflict here. One is equality at the individual level—as understod in the concept of equal protection of the law. The second is an aggregate equality which seeks to equalize conditions within the society overall. Frequently the goal of aggregate equality compromises the desire for equal treatment. This dilemma is expressed very clearly by Ronald Dworkin, analyzing the issues in the *DeFunis* v. *Odegaard* case on preferential law school admissions for minorities:

There is nothing paradoxical, of course, in the idea that an individual's right to equal protection may sometimes conflict with an otherwise desirable social policy, including the policy of making the community more equal overall.... [The *DeFunis* case] forces us to acknowledge the distinction between equality as a policy and equality as a right, a distinction that political theory has virtually ignored. [DeFunis] argues that the Washington law school violated the individual right to equality for the sake of a policy of greater equality overall.[24]

The search for a solution to this dilemma returns our attention to the earlier question of the realtion of equality to other values; we were concerned with whether equality as a value was always preeminent and nonnegotiable or whether it should be balanced against other values. Now our dilemma is more subtle and even more difficult. We find that there are various kinds of equality which may come into conflict with each other. Policy makers must determine how important is equal protection for the individual, compared with aggregate equality. One can no longer simply say that equality is preeminent, but must specify the kind of equality so considered and recognize the costs to other forms of equality. Again, we are confronted with the implications of a very ambiguous concept and of its serious, often conflicting, implications for public choice.

This chapter began with the suggestion that everything to be said about equality might already have been said. We conclude on a much less settled note. It now seems that equality is such an elusive concept that we cannot talk seriously about equality without talking about what is essential to human nature. But talk about human "essences" is unsatisfying and unsettling to those with an empirical turn of mind, as well as to those under pressure of making day-to-day hard policy decisions. We must find a way to bridge the gap between philosophical discourse and public choice. There must be a way to incorporate the best available knowledge from the biological and social sciences into our philosophical conceptions and at the same time render those conceptions relevant to public decisions.

Furthermore, we have found it difficult to talk about equality as a value without talking about what it means to value and how we justify our value choices. In this area philosophers have developed highly sophisticated arguments regarding the grounds and the logic of evaluation, but they have frequently failed to translate these arguments into the language of public policy. What is needed is a systematic and rigorous analysis of the ethical arguments underlying public policies pertaining to equality.

Finally, and perhaps most frustrating to advocates of equality, is the fact that we cannot even be sure that we are treating people equally because there are so many diverse facets to any interaction. Equal treatment in one facet of a social interaction may necessarily imply unequal treatment in another facet. Still, the complexities of arguing about equality should not lead us to despair of ever achieving the goal of equal treatment. Complexity should not breed paralysis (nor should it supply an excuse for turning away from greater equality). Rather, these complexities should lead us to consider the pervasive issues in which equality is embedded, and increase our concern for and attention to the intellectual processes by which we reach principled decisions.

9

Hobson's Choice and the
Political Economy of Equality in America

James C. Foster

Right can never be higher than the economic structure of society
and the cultural development thereby determined.

Karl Marx
Critique of the Gotha Program

The best way...to make sense of the belief in equality is to watch
how those who espouse it deal with human differences.... Individuals obviously vary. The issue is how we view these differences and
what actions we decided to make consequent upon them.

Andrew Hacker
Creating American Inequality

At the conclusion of chapter 8 we urged that the complexities of arguing about
equality should not lead us to despair of achieving the goal of equal treatment.
Our concern, expressed there, is that heightened sophistication with regard to
equality as a social issue should not retard, but rather serve to advance equality in
America. Awareness of life's complexities is no reason for faint-heartedness. In
this chapter we argue on behalf of fundamental economic change as a prerequisite
to achieving greater equality in the United States. As such, this chapter is a
demonstration of our belief that principled argument in support of equality not
only is possible, but that it must be undertaken to further equality.

Contemporary debates about equality in the United States revolve around two
seemingly opposed positions. Those whom we would characterize as reform
liberals tend to support the achievement of equality through government action:
affirmative action, expanded social service programs such as federally assisted
housing and Head Start, full-employment acts, and the like. Those currently

termed neoconservatives[1] advocate much less government intervention, many arguing that inequality has proven virtually impervious to government programs established in lieu of market (free enterprise) approaches, others holding that equality is tantamount to a leveling which threatens values such as merit and efficiency. Typically, these two positions are perceived by Americans as being diametrically opposed to each other as well as comprising the last words on equality.

This chapter contends, in part, that such perceptions blind us to weaknesses in both positions and preclude our serious consideration of alternative visions. It argues against the assumption underlying opposition between reform liberals and neoconservatives—that, taken together, they offer Americans a viable choice about equality. In our view, although they are different, both positions misunderstand equality and both positions give us policy programs that are seriously flawed. In this way, our society finds itself in a situation strikingly similar to that of customers in Thomas Hobson's seventeenth-century stable: the apparent choices are in fact no choice at all.[2] Americans have confined themselves strictly to the policy options of either *gesturing on behalf of equality* by pumping relatively small amounts of money and large amounts of bureaucracy into society, or *forsaking equality* in the name of "realism" by abandoning people to the exigencies of an economy managed for private profit. Thus our Hobson's choice: be swallowed up in red tape or fend for ourselves in a world of corporate capital.

Equality is a relatively recent addition to the public policy agenda in the United States. To be sure, equality plays a salient role in our political tradition. We saw, in section 1, the roots of American equality in the writings of John Locke and Thomas Hobbes. Prominent mention was made of equality as part of the moral basis for our Declaration of Independence, which severed our colonial ties with England. Throughout American history eloquent support has been paid to equality in the abstract. While all this is true, American actions—and inactions—seem to belie effective commitment. It was not until blacks demanded an end to the most egregious form of inequality, racism, and mobilized to enforce that demand that even halting steps were undertaken to live up to generations of lofty rhetoric. In response primarily to the civil rights movement, preliminary, tentative measures were undertaken to realize the promise of equality. Rights of ethnic minorities, of women, the aged, children, the handicapped, and the poor were recognized as a consequence of the many fights that had been joined. In addition to these formal, legal claims, specific programs such as those examined in section 2 were initiated in order to make rights realities. It looked as though some advances, meager as they might have been, were taking place.

Then came the 1970s. More specifically, came economic decline and political retrenchment. In his recent book, *Inequality in an Age of Decline,* Paul Blumberg captures the essence of our changed economic conditions:

In the early 1960s President Kennedy spoke of America on a New Frontier. By the 1970s America was, indeed, on a new frontier, but one radically different from the one Kennedy had in mind. It was a frontier of economic crisis unlike anything America had ever experienced before: unprecedented inflation, high unemployment, a precipitously declining dollar, enormous trade deficits, the rapid erosion of the U.S. technological lead, declining productivity growth, and loss of control over vital energy sources. While America had experienced some of these problems before (unemployment, inflation), their simultaneous combination was entirely new.[3]

Economic decline bought political retrenchment. With the Nixon administration's perfunctory reiteration of reform slogans and its actual perpetration of illegality and injustice, the goal of equality, only recently adopted, was initially scaled down as too ambitious, then shelved as politically unpopular. The subsequent Carter administration's "go slow" approach under the twin banners of realism and moderation was nothing other than a rehashed version of Nixon/ Ford's generally reduced efforts. Indeeed, the rush of former Great Society supporters to embrace neoconservatism is symptomatic of the American political elite's less-than-full support for equality in the first place and their consequent severe susceptibility to disappointment. Our point here is not the fashionable one put forward these days that equality is inappropriate or impossible, but rather that too many policy makers and opinion shapers have rejected it all too easily. In the manner of a self-fulfilling prophecy, reduced efforts on behalf of equality gave rise to the conviction that it cannot and, in the extreme case, ought not to be achieved. Frustration followed, and justified, prior retreat.

The present situation poses a danger and an opportunity for Americans. The danger lies in the prospect that the struggle for equality in the United States will be lost either through lack of understanding of the concept or by default. On the other hand, we seen an opportunity inhering in the possibility of rethinking equality and proceeding with new resolve. This chapter seeks to further realization of this opportunity by accomplishing two tasks: theoretically analyzing the concept of human equality in order to understand what it entails, and critically surveying various strategies in order to learn how best to achieve genuine human equality. As we will see, the real choice facing this country with regard to equality is not between more or less government intervention, but between the perpetuation of inequality or fuller knowledge about the qualities of being equal coupled with fundamental economic change.

This choice is suggested to us by the point of view adopted here, which may be characterized variously as Marxist, socialist, or critical. While perhaps not inaccurate, all these labels are by themselves too vague and far too freighted with misapprehensions to define adequately what this chapter seeks to accomplish. The term radical political economy probably comes closest to capturing the principles and conceptual framework which inform the following analysis. Understood to be synonymous with what economist Howard Sherman calls nondogmtic Marxism, radical political economy seeks to join understanding with action. Its method is analysis of existing conditions, placing emphasis on interconnections, conflict among interests of owners and nonowners of capital, and change.[4] Its purpose—our purpose in this chapter—is to advocate changes in the existing structure of things in order to further human liberation. Of necessity, this requires a tone of advocacy. As Sherman explains:

No social scientist is unbiased; all come from a particular social environment, and all have tentative conclusions (conscious or unconscious) on any issue they are investigating. . . .

Moreover, a social science that presented no conclusions would be useless. Imagine an engineer who tells us there are ten different ways to build the bridge we are considering, but refuses to tell us which he believes best under the circumstances (admitting that further knowledge may change his judgment in the future).[5]

This chapter, then, represents the union of explanation with prescription. The radicalism of this approach consists of delving into the roots—the material basis—of contemporary concepts of equality and policy toward equality in order to overcome deficiencies inherent in the reform liberal and neoconservative positions. Our awareness of the problematical nature of such an endeavor is matched by our belief that critical examination of orthodoxy—in both its reform liberal and neoconservative manifestations—is of the utmost importance. Michael Best and William Connolly express our sentiments:

Since a growing number of people suspect that the established ideas do not adequately explain the established system, we trust our ideas will be given attention. We are not certain that our interpretation is true, but we think it is on the right track. And we know that no one can assess the worth of prevailing ideas without seriously exploring at least one theory [radical political economy] that challenges the assumptions hidden inside those established beliefs and ideals.[6]

Prior to proceeding with our critique of reform liberal and neoconservative strategies vis-a-vis equality, it is necessary to comment preliminarily on their shared fundamental failure to comprehend the qualities of being equal as those qualities pertain to humans. We will return to discuss socialist equality in greater detail later in the chapter. Our concern here is to point out that both reform liberals and neoconservatives rest their strategies toward equality on certain flawed assumptions. They basically misapprehend what it means for humans to be equal.

Regardless of their party affiliation, most Americans derive their concept of equality from contemporary liberal-capitalism, which associates being equal with external attributes. By this we mean that most Americans associate being equal with having similar possessions, similar status, similar wealth. Thorstein Veblen captured the essence of this understanding of equality in his classic analysis of pecuniary emulation:

In order to stand well in the eyes of the community, it is necessary to come up to a certain, somewhat indefinite, conventional standard of wealth.... Those members of the community who fall short of this, somewhat indefinite, normal degree of...property suffer in the esteem of their fellow-men; and consequently they suffer also in their own esteem since the usual basis of self-respect is the respect accorded by one's neighbors.[7]

We have termed this conception proprietary equality. It defines being equal in terms of what one *has* rather than by what one *is*. Equality, according to this notion, is epitomized by a leveling of things, rewards, and experiences.

Ironically, proprietary equality runs directly counter to an alternative conceptualization well known (at least rhetorically) to almost all Americans. We refer here, of course, to the view articulated by our Declaration of Independence: "We hold these truths to be self-evident, that all men are created equal. . . ." The clear implication of Jefferson's wording is that equality is not a condition humans achieve, but that it is inherent in being human. In contrast to the liberal-capitalist notion of proprietary equality, we would term this alternative an innate or ontological equality. In this view, human beings are equal beings—equal in worth, in dignity, and in their capacity for moral judgment.

Now, we are well aware of the essential nonconfirmability of ontological equality. We are aware as well, as we pointed out in the previous chapter, that such inherent lack of verification will cause the strict empiricists among our readers discomfort. We want to emphasize—for the benefit of all readers—that our concern with positing ontological equality revolves around the *consequences* which flow from this premise in contrast to those resulting from proprietary equality. It matters less to us that we cannot prove ontological equality than that such a premise is conducive to human welfare in ways that proprietary equality is not. Ontological equality gives rise to valuing human differences. Proprietary equality gives rise to "invidious comparison," to quote Veblen again. We agree with Andrew Hacker who, after tracing the tradition we call here ontological equality, writes:

Such differences as we do note [between humans] can simply acknowledge variation, without overtones of "inequality." A parent with three children may remark on their different traits and temperaments, yet refrain from ranking one any higher than another. "Inequality" comes into being when we begin to talk of higher, better, superior. And that was a temptation these writers wished us to avoid. Such disparate thinkers as Hobbes and Hume and Rousseau could agree that there are many kinds of talents, that intelligence comes in varied forms. But they were not ready to say that one person's mind or sphere of competence should be ranked superior to another's.[8]

We will return below to examine the relationship between ontological equality and the socialist concept of equality. For now, our point is that understanding equality in ontological terms requires treating human beings profoundly differently than does proprietary equality.

Some wag once characterized American reform liberals as people incapable of arriving at the conclusions their own analyses lead them to embrace. Although there is humor to be had at their expense, the plight of American reformers (not to mention the plight of those whose disadvantages are perpetuated as a consequence of reform liberal failures) has no little tragedy to it. At one level, the fallacy in the reform liberals' approach to equality is their failure to realize that corporate capitalism is the source of unacceptable inequalities in the United States. Equality is clearly incompatible with a system of production which holds the pursuit of self-interest as the chief purpose in life. Blind to this basic contradiction, reform liberals cannot perceive the larger pattern woven by their disconnected analyses of American social problems. Poor housing, inadequate health care, estranging education, malnutrition, perennial gaps in wealth and income between men and women, rich and poor, blacks and whites—reform liberals perceive these social problems in discrete instead of holistic terms. Incapable of seeing the forest for the trees, reform liberals embrace strategies that are incremental, meliorative at most, and supportive of the basic causes of inequality in the long run.

The reform liberal approach to the maldistributiion of wealth and income in the United States serves to illustrate the impotence of that strategy. To begin with, reform liberals misdiagnose the cause of such maldistribution. Instead of discerning the ways corporate capitalism creates stratification by concentrating greater and greater wealth and power in fewer and fewer interests, they have resorted to a hodgepodge of government programs (New Deal, Fair Deal, New Frontier, Great Society), collectively insufficient to treat even the symptoms of advanced capitalism, much less the disease itself. The notion of "reform" in the American context implies a primary commitment to *strengthening* the existence of capitalism by means of timely adjustments: regulating the economic system so that it "serves" the people, managing people in such a manner that they serve the economic sysem. Interpreted in these terms, the reform liberals' essential concern is conservative in the sense of perpetuating capitalism. By most accounts, their record has been highly successful: they have firmly established and legitimated corporate capitalism by retarding its cycles and smoothing its more damaging consequences.

Political scientist Edward Greenberg characterizes this success as the result of "the conservative uses of liberal reform." Summarizing the consequences of almost fifty years of reforming, Greenberg writes:

The Age of Reform [1890-1939] was really an effort by leading members of the business community to bring order, stability, and predictability to the competitive chaos of the emerging industrial order, to incorporate labor into the business system through conservative unionism, and to prevent social revolution through the distribution of minimal relief benefits to the poor. The Age of Reform was essentially a series of reforms designed to ensure the dominance and profitability of large-scale capital and to blunt movements for radical alternatives to the status quo.[9]

In their concern to shore up capitalism, reform liberals—political descendants of the venturous conservatives—have consistently directed their energies toward the problem of distribution: how to divide up the pie. In fact, inequality in America cannot be substantially eroded without attention to the problems of production and ownership as well: the substance and control of the pie. Political economists Best and Connolly write that reform liberals experiment with "job training for the unemployed, expansion of welfare programs, a negative income tax to provide income floors for those at the bottom of the system, and most ambitiously, a graduated income tax that would significantly close the gap between high- and low-income earners." The common failing of this approach, continue Best and Connolly, is that it leaves "the system of ownership and production untouched." Reform liberals "seek to reform the system of distribution without altering the system of production in which it is anchored."[10]

The nature of that system of production is inherently unequal. Referring to the bias of capitalist production in his *Critique of the Gotha Program,* Marx argued:

The capitalist mode of production, for example, rests on the fact that the material conditions of production are in the hands of non-workers in the form of property in capital and land, while the masses are only owners of the personal condition of production, viz., labour power. Once the elements of production are so distributed, then the present day distribution of the means of consumption results automatically. If the material conditions of production are the co-operative property of the workers themselves, then this likewise results in a different distribution of the means of consumption from the present one.[11]

The implications of Marx's analysis for equality and equity should be clear: as long as the *ownership* of the means of production is unequally distributed, the resulting distribution of what is produced will remain unequal. In concrete terms, this means that "at the upper end of the distribution [of wealth and income in the United States], property income accruing to the capitalist class is the primary source of inequality." While there are many sources of inequality in wealth and income in America, race, sex, educational, and regional differences among them, the "primary source of high incomes...is ownership of income producing property."[12] In spite of this fact, reform liberals pay little heed to revising the structure of ownership in this society.

At a related level, reform liberals fail to understand that those without capital—"workers" in the most inclusive sense of the term[13]—are *equally dependent* upon selling their labor power for survival. This situation is the other side of the capitalist coin from what was described just above: those who own the means of production enjoy equal advantages while those who do not own suffer equal disadvantage.[14] More specifically, the nature of this disadvantage is having one's survival depend upon working on terms defined by the pursuit of private profit. The character of this subjugation to capitalist rules of the game can be illustrated by reference to what Marx termed the commodity-form. At the outset of *Capital* Marx writes, "The wealth of those societies in which the capitalist mode of production prevails, presents itself as 'an immense accumulation of commodities,' its unit being a single commodity."[15] Marx began *Capital* in this way because he understood that commodities were at the heart of the capitalist mode of production. The essence of a commodity, for Marx, is its value in exchange: what it will bring to its owner. Commodities are the embodiment of wealth in a capitalist society, and primary among all commodities is human labor power—the physical and mental abilities of all "those who work for capital in various ways in exchange for a portion of the total social wealth they produce."[16]

The commodity-form thus defines the relationship between owners and non-owners of capital. It specifies the terms under which most of us work in a capitalist society: the system in which a worker sells a part of himself, as the commodity labor power, in return for the historically and socially variable means of survival. Economist Harry Cleaver summarizes this relationship:

The overwhelming majority of the people are put in a situation where they are forced to work to avoid starvation. The capitalist class creates and maintains this situation of compulsion by achieving total control over all the means of producing social wealth. The generalized imposition of the commodity-form has meant that forced work has become the fundamental means of organizing society—of social control. It means the creation of a working class—a class of people who can survive only by selling their capacity to work to the class that controls the means of production.... The commodity-form is thus a set of power relations.[17]

In this light, capitalist equality means equal subjugation to the commodity-form. Needless to say, reform liberals rarely conceive of change in terms of reforming this particular sort of equality.

It is not only with regard to the structure of capitalist ownership and production that reform liberal analyses of America's social ills fail. Across the board, reformist social policies based upon marginal readjustments in the nature of distribution founder time and again. As Christopher Jencks et al. put it at the conclusion of their sobering analysis of the effects of schooling in the United States on inequality, "As long as egalitarians assume that public policy cannot contribute to economic equality directly but must proceed by ingenuous manipulations of marginal institutions like the schools, progress will remain glacial."[18] As contemporary American politics makes quite clear, such a glacial pace fuels frustration and disillusionment among the disadvantaged while, at the same time, putting weapons in the hands of those opposed to any changes whatsoever.

Michael Harrington, the man largely responsible for calling Americans' attention to the poverty in our midst in his *The Other America,* has analyzed how reform liberal policies, when enacted into law, seem to harm the very disadvantaged they were supposed to aid. His explanation emphasizes how the class-oriented assumptions of reform sabotage its intentions:

How...can we explain why sincere and dedicated men—as those who presided over these disastrous [housing] programs usually were—would lavish public funds to thus aggravate social problems? The answer is to be found in the class character of American society and the commercial logic which both derives from it and pervades governmental decisions.... For in a society based upon class inequality and suffused with commercial values, it just doesn't "make sense" to waste resources on social uses or beauty or anything that cannot be quantified in dollars and cents. Our legislators, drawn almost exclusvely from the middle and upper classes, cannot bring themselves to forget those principles, which are sacred to the private economy. To them it seems logical to invest the Federal dollar in those undertakings that run the lowest risk and will show the highest and most immediate return.[19]

From the perspective of radial political economy, not only is the welfare state imbued with the logic and values of capital, it is dependent upon the vitality of capital for its very survival. As Harrington writes in *The Twilight of Capitalism:*

The welfare-state government is not itself the initiator of most production within the economy. The corporations do that. However, the same government is increasingly charged with arranging the preconditions for profitable production. Its funds, its power, its political survival, depend on private-sector performance. So do the jobs of most workers. The state's interest in perpetuating its own rule is thus, in economic fact, identified with the health of the capitalist economy.... The essential fact is that the capitalist state is not itself capitalist: It therefore depends on capitalists.[20]

Many examples could be cited to illustrate the failings of reform liberal social policies. We will take up two: medical care and environmental protection.

Health care in America is premised upon the same principles and logic as most other services: tied to the commodity form, i.e., supplied in exchange for money, it is subject to differences in wealth and income. While it is difficult to imagine a service more essential to human well-being and thus *public* in the sense that health maintenance concerns us all, medical care in the United States is generally supplied through *private* providers on the basis of fee-for-service. As Edward Greenberg writes, "Medical care is exchanged for money, and the people without adequate finances are left with the dredges of what is, at best, a barely adequate health system."[21] Greenberg elaborates on this situation:

There is no foolproof way to explain the wide disparities in health among the population in the United States. However, two explanations stand out from the many possibilities: (1) the commodity nature of health care, and (2) the human pathology of social class. One of the principal problems of health care distribution in the United States is that such care is considered not a right of all citizens, but something that is bought and sold in the marketplace. Doctors are, by and large, professionals who sell their services to those who can afford to pay the bill.... It goes almost without saying that those with the greatest disposable income will be those for whom the medical profession is most solicitous. Just as the poor and the near poor have limited access to the goods and services of American life, so too are they denied access to the best in medical care.... The result is that "how long a person will live, the disease he will have, the type of treatment he will receive, and the cause of his death are strongly influenced by the amount of money there is to spend on health."[22]

Since our illustration pertains to health care, we will couch our conclusion in terms of a medical analogy: with regard to the pathology of unequal access to medical care in America, reform liberals persistently treat the disease's symptoms, enacting such programs as Medicare and Medicaid, which provide some money and much paperwork and which neglect the disease's cause rooted in the commodification of medical services. As a palliative, money is an indicator of the fallacy of tying provision of medical care to the cash nexus; money itself is neither a cause nor a cure. Human need rather than effective demand must become the basis for providing medical care before artificial *inequalities of access* to physicians' services will be replaced by natural *inequalities of use.*[23]

At first glance, the issue of environmental protection seems unconnected with the matter of equality. The connection, nevertheless, is intimate and crucial. Reform liberals, since they subscribe to the logic of capital, also subscribe to its logic of growth. Barry Weisberg describes this logic:

"All natural relationships have been dissolved into money relationships." Today the ownership of property and capital is equivalent to the ownership of the environment itself. The concentration of production and capital, of industrial capital with banking capital, the increasing rise of exports over imports, the increasing production of surplus in relation to total product (waste)—all combine in the ultimate concentration of the multinational corporation. In its consumate development, capitalism requires constantly accelerating levels of consumption, rising productivity, and *the impulse to accumulate for its own sake.* Marx called it the circulation of capital. We call it growth.[24]

The connection between capitalist equality and environmental degradation is implicit in Weisberg's description of capitalist growth. The logic runs that equality is solely a function of accumulation, accumulation is a function of expanding consumption, expanding consumption requires expanding productivity, expanding productivity is the result of unrestrained capital. In this manner, greater equality is established over against greater environmentl protection. Jobs or ecology, as the conventional wisdom has it.

The core of the problem according to the French political economist Andre Gorz, is the failure of many (including many contemporary Marxists) to recognize that human equality is not the result of what we understand by affluence, defined in terms of the categories of more and less. Only liberal-capitalist notions of equality require comparing ourselves on the basis of our possessions. Writes Gorz:

This is what lies behind the unending pursuit of an ever-receding equality: those in each income category seek parity with those at the next level of income who, in turn, attempt to "catch up" with those above them. Beyond a certain level, increases in income are sought not for their own sake or for the additional consumption which they represent. Interestingly, they reflect above all the demand that society recognize us as having the same rights, the same standing, and social value we see attributed to others. In a society based on the unequal remuneration of jobs equally devoid of meaning, the demand for equality is the hidden source of the continuing escalation of consumer demand, dissatisfaction, and social competitiveness.

Preserving environmental integrity requires stabilization of consumption; with regard to achieving this goal, Gorz concludes:

The stabilization of the level of consumption will thus remain impossible until:
—all socially necessary tasks receive equal social recognition (and rewards) and
—the possibility is given to everyone to actualize the infinite diversity of abilities, desires, and personal tastes through an unlimited variety of free individual and collective activities. . . .
Different standards of living and lifestyles will cease to signify inequality when they are the result not of differences in income but of the diversity of pursuits by communities and individuals during their free time.[25]

In sum, Gorz's argument is that, short of stabilizing our level of consumption, pollution, waste, and destruction will continue to bulk large in American life. Equality is thereby intimately tied up with environmental protection: until the call of defenders and reformers of the status quo alike—more for everyone!—is replaced by respect for human rights, standing, and value, the pursuit of equality can only undermine our environment.

Turning from the reform liberal camp to that of the neoconservatives, we develop the feeling of being between a rock and a hard place. As political scientist Walter Dean Burnham noted toward the end of a recent article on American politics in the 1980s, Americans are confronted with "an ongoing, increasingly sterile debate between laissez-faire conservatives and 'statist' liberals."[26] If reform liberal strategies effectively stand as Scylla, a rock in the path toward enlarged human equality in America, the consequences of neoconservative proposals would certainly resemble Charybdis. In our view, while reform liberal policy suggestions stymie achievement of genuine equality, neoconservative alternatives would effectively curtail what achievements we have gained by abandoning Americans to the exigencies of a domestic, albeit multinational, economy managed for private profit in a world that is growing increasingly difficult to profit from.

The neoconservatives' failure with regard to equality has three dimensions. First, neoconservatives maintain a negative view of politics and an idealized view of economics respectively, and misunderstand the relationship between them. They conceive of politics as largely confined to government and of government as the realm of coercion. Economics, on the other hand, is viewed synonymously with markets and thus is the realm of free choice. Second, neoconservatives support inequality as functional in that it carries out the socially necessary task of allocating scarce resources on the basis of required occupations. For them, equality is dysfunctional, hence, disadvantageous in a complex, industrial society such as ours. Third and most fundamentally, neoconservatives misunderstand what human equality entails. Variously conceiving of equality in terms of "leveling," "equality of results," or "sameness," they reject equality as inefficient, subversive of merit, and conducive to conformity. We elaborate on each of these failings below.

There are two parts to our argument that neoconservatives hold negative, idealized views of politics and economics. The initial part concerns the manner in which they define "politics" and "economics" respectively. Government is the source of our problems, neoconservatives are apt to say; or, at least, it is not the source of solutions to societal problems. In saying this, neoconservatives imply that politics, as well, is a source of our problems instead of solutions. In short, the typical neoconservative argument identifies politics, i.e., the activity or ordering our lives, with government, and is suspicious of both. Such a conception blurs some very important distinctions and blinds us to basic facts.

To begin with, assuming that politics is synonymous with domination and that government is synonymous with politics involves embracing a position that holds politics and government to be primarily about invidious control or, as political scientist Robert Dahl put it in his widely cited formulation: "*A* has power over *B* to the extent that he can get *B* to do something that *B* would not otherwise do."[27] The situation Dahl defines is often erroneously taken to be a simple case of coercion as, for example, in the pat conservative phrase "Government meddles too much in the free market." This position assumes a dichotomy between government coercion and economic choice. There are at least two serious problems with this view: the exercise of power involves considerably more than coercion; and coercion is not confined solely to the public sector. Power over others has many dimensions, and it is just as characteristic of American economic life (perhaps more so) as of political life. That Exxon, for example, wields great economic power is a virtual truism the truth of which is nevertheless vitiated by talk of paternalism in government in contrast to the free market.

Additionally, it is important to understand that government—the apparatus of the state—is distinct from, although clearly related to, politics. Politics is the *activity* by which different societies order (rule) their affairs. Politics, as C. Wright Mills might have put it, is the mediating activity between personal lives and social history.[28] Defined in part by culturally specific configurations of values, attitudes, and beliefs, in part by structurally specific configurations of ownership, production, and control politics determines the nature of government. This distinction between politics and government is not an academic one. Its upshot is that the character of the American state (government) is a function of the politics of an advanced capitalist society. Perceived in this light, we can see that the neoconservatives are partially correct and basically wrong: they realize that government is not the solution to our problem with regard to achieving greater equality, yet they neglect the promise of politics in lieu of professing "considerable respect for the market as an instrument for allocating resources efficiently while preserving individual freedom."[29] We have more to say below about the promise of politics.

While progress toward equality may not result from government tinkering, we are convinced that it certainly will not come from giving more rein to the American market. It will not come because the American market is dominated by monopoly capital: "Monopoly capitalism developed out of the preceding stage of capitalism ('competitive capitalism') with the emergence in the advanced capitalist countries of huge agglomerations of capital. These immense concentrations took various forms as corporations, trusts, cartels, financial groups, conglomerates, and muiltinationals."[30] Cherished American myths to the contrary notwithstanding, it is a fact of our daily lives that our economic system has not responded to the dictates of sovereign consumers in a free market since before the dawn of the twentieth century. Instead, the American economy is managed for private profit.

This situation was analyzed more than fifteen years ago by Michael Reagan. In Reagan's words, what exists in America is a "system of corporate administration of resources." He argues:

Conscious human management is replacing the market as the basic allocator of resources, distributor of income, and stabilizer of employment and production.... The automatic economy is dead. "The managed economy" is the phrase that applies to both the public and the private sectors, and it also indicates the specific quality of the mixed economy: that both elements are managed.[31]

One neoconservative, Daniel Bell, appears to agree with Reagan's analysis. In his *The Coming of Post-Industrial Society,* Bell clearly acknowledges the managed economy: "A post industrial society...is increasingly a communal society wherein public mechanisms rather than the market become the allocators of goods, and public choice, rather than individual demand, becomes the arbiter of services."[32] The difference between Reagan and Bell hinges on the interests which such management reflects. In other words, the crucial question is: If our economy is managed, toward what ends is it manipulated? Bell's reply is that the economy serves society through government: "if the major historic turn in the last quarter of a century has been the subordination of economic function to societal goals, the political order [government] necessarily becomes the control system of the society."[33] Reagan's analysis leads him to draw a different conclusion:

In short, profit-making still counts; institutional survival is the overriding criterion. When welfare or cultural expenditures are seen as "paying off," they will be undertaken. When they conflict with profit, they will be passed by.... The corporate conscience is, then, a self-interested conscience and hardly a reliable vehicle for achieving the common good. It cannot work, at least not in the way asserted by the proponents of social trusteeship.[34]

Reagan's argument leads us to suggest that, instead of extolling the efficiency of an idealized market or celebrating the fanciful subordination of private to social goals in a managed economy, neoconservatives should fix their attentions upon the relationship between capitalist production and inequality. If coercion is largely a consequence of what President Franklin D. Roosevelt referred to as necessitous[35] lives, then coercion is not primarily a result of government intervention in the marketplace but of the systematic ways in which advanced capitalism denies basic needs to poor Americans while debasing the needs of most Americans. In this regard, we agree with Andre Gorz when he writes:

Economic, cultural, and social development are not oriented toward the development of human beings and the satisfaction of their social needs as a priority, but *first* toward the creation of those articles which can be sold with the maximum profit, regardless of their utility or lack of utility. Creative activity is limited by the criteria of financial profitability or of social stability, while millions of hours of work are wasted in the framework of monopoly competition in order to incorporate modifications in consumer products, modifications which are often marginal but always costly, and which aim at increasing neither the use value nor the esthetic value of the product.... Mature capitalist society, therefore, remains profoundly barbaric as a *society,* to the degree that it aims at no civilization of social existence and of social relationships, no culture of social individuals, but only a civilization of individual consumption.[36]

The second failing of neoconservative arguments with regard to equality is their embrace of inequality. Too much equality (as they understand the phenomenon) is a bad thing. Daniel Bell, for instance, despairs over what he calls a Tocqueville effect,[37] whereby Americans have become committed to leveling all differences, to the disadvantage of motivation and excellence. We are in danger of arriving at the point, Bell maintains, where equality threatens more important American values as well as the stability of our society. Nathan Glazer, the late Martin Diamond, Daniel Moynihan, Aaron Wildavsky, Irving Kristol, Robert Nisbet, Norman Podhoretz—seemingly all neoconservatives join Robert Nisbet in decrying the new equality as giving rise to a new despotism.

One argument put forward to defend inequality maintains that equality can be encouraged only to the extent that it does not interfere with the necessary task of encouraging qualified individuals to occupy society's crucial occupational roles. In other words, it is argued that inequality serves the vital function of matching competent persons with required positions; a function essential to the maintenance of a complex division of labor.

Perhaps the most sophisticated version of this ideology of inequality is functionalism. Drawing on the work of sociologists Kingsley Davis and Wilbert Moore, Michael Best and William Connolly provide an overview of the theory:

Every society...must first distribute its members into the various jobs or roles defined by the society and then motivate them to perform their tasks efficiently. Some roles or positions are more important than others in the sense that the successful performance of them is crucial to the welfare of the whole society. In addition, some tasks require skills that are either difficult or scarce because they require a good deal of special training. In order to ensure that the most important and difficult tasks are performed competently, every society rewards the performance of these tasks highly. The system of unequal rewards thereby functions as a set of incentives to channel the most competent people into the most important and difficult roles and then ensures that they will perform these tasks efficiently. The greater the division of labor in society, the greater the range must be between the positions with the lowest rewards and those with the highest.[38]

Functionalism, at first glance, appears highly persuasive; so much so, in fact, that it is treated as common sense by most Americans. Despite this fact, functionalism is subject to several telling challenges which can be summarized as follows:[39] (1) On the basis of what criteria does a society assess the relative importance of the skills it requires? Who formulates these criteria? Is widespread participation in the assessment process assured merely by the fact that such assessment is necessary? (2) If the relative scarcity of skills is the primary criterion determining the level of rewards, how does society guarantee that artificial scarcity is not created by those who exercise market power? In other words, how is society to distinguish between genuine and contrived scarcity, assuring that the latter will not be rewarded? (3) Functionalism includes, although this is seldom emphasized, negative sanctions as well as positive rewards. On the basis of its own assumptions that rewards must be given in relation to the possession of scarce and/or important skills, "the carrot at higher levels requires the stick at lower levels." (4) Functionalism deals exclusively in external, individualistic incentives, assuming that they are universal and singular. Might not internal, social incentives, coupled with more conventional rewards, restructure the workplace and cause less invidious inequality? (5) For those on the bottom of society, functionalism results in the double jeopardy of having to believe not only in the legitimacy of the reward structure but in one's personal responsibility for his or her plight. In this manner, functionalism creates a self-fulfilling prophecy: self-congratulatory for the haves, self-destructive for the have-nots.

In an ironic way inequality *is* functional in the United States, but not in the ways functionalists describe. The functions of poverty have less to do with matching people with roles than with the maintenance of the capitalist status quo. The work of Herbert Gans and information derived from an article in *U.S. News & World Report* shed revealing light on the nature of these functions.

Among the thirteen economic, political, and ideological "uses" of poverty[40] that Gans cites are these:

(1) the existence of poverty ensures that society's "dirty work" will be done; (2) the very low wages of the poor subsidize a variety of economic activities that benefit the affluent (domestic servants, for instance), and the poor pay a disproportionate share of all taxes; (3) poverty creates jobs for middle-class people who "serve" the poor, such as social workers, prison guards, and so on; (4) the poor buy goods that others wouldn't, which is profitable to those who produce and sell them.

Other uses of poverty, according to Gans, range from its enhancement of middle class moral and social standing, to providing available recruits for the military in time of war.

The *U.S. News & World Report* article adds a necessary dimension to Gans's analysis. It could be argued, without contradicting Gans's conclusions, that even though poverty fulfills the functions mentioned above, it is caused by the individual shortcomings, cultural deprivation, and/or other pathologies of the poor themselves. the *U.S. News* article effectively refutes this claim. Of particular interest are the following pieces of information:[41] Poor people who are physically capable of working but do not hold jobs amount to only 12 percent of all disadvantaged. Of this 12 percent, only 1.5 percent are able-bodied males. Fully 25 percent of the poor hold jobs but earn so little that they are unable to get above the poverty line. Of the remaining poor, most are children, mothers with small children, older adults, and handicapped. In the face of these facts and others belying myths about the indolent poor, *U.S. News* quotes the strikingly understated conclusion of the business-oriented Conference Board: "Unraveling the problems of the unemployed and the marginally employed is now seen to be a longer-term and much more difficult and risky enterprise that it was originally thought."[42]

It should be emphasized that we are not arguing that inequality could or should be totally abolished from our society. We are trying to distinguish between *essential* inequalities and *artificial* invidious inequalities. It is one thing to argue that some differentials in reward structures must exist to ensure that necessary roles are filled and carried out with efficiency. We agree with this in principle, although we point out the various ways and means of implementing such differentials. Our disagreement is not with such functional differences but with functionalism: the ideological use of needed differentials to justify invidious inequalities. Although some inequality is inevitable, the issue is *which inequalities are defensible and which are not?* John Schaar raises this issue:

Certainly, some things *are* better than others, and more to be preferred. Some vocations and talents are more valuable than others, and more to be rewarded. My argument here is only that the more highly skilled, trained, or talented man has no ground either for thinking himself a better *man* that his less-favored fellows, or for regarding his superiorities as providing any but the most temporary and limited justification for authority over others. The paradigmatic case is that of the relation between teacher and student. The teacher's superior knowledge gives him a just claim to authority over his students. But central to the ethic of teaching is the conviction that the teacher must impart to students not only his substantive knowledge but also the critical skills and habits necessary for judging and contributing to that knowledge. The teacher justifies his authority and fulfills his duty by making himself unnecessary to the student.[43]

Of course, Schaar's justification of inequality is rooted in a very different notion of equality than that embraced by most Americans. His ontological conception of equality does not so much reject human differences, role specialization, and reward differentials as place them in the context of fundamental human dignity and equal availability of those goods and services required to support human dignity. As this notion is lost, not merely on neoconservatives but on the majority of Americans, when we indict the former, thirdly, for failure to understand what genuine human equality entails, we simply single them out as a specific instance of a more general failing.

With regard to equality, neoconservative fears have several dimensions: equality versus liberty, equality versus meritocracy, equality versus legitimacy.[44] All these are various expressions of a single fear, nevertheless, and that is fear of leveling—social, political, and economic leveling. Animating all the neoconservative watchwords—"Tocqueville effect," "revolution of equality," "new equality," "egalitarian precipice"—is an assumption that equality is tantamount to bringing everyone down to the lowest common denominator. In a word, equality is assumed to be equal to sameness. Now, to the extent that this assumption functions as a straw man erected for purposes of winning debating points against liberal opponents, it can be dismissed as crafty or cynical or both. To the extent that such an assumption accurately reflects the level at which Americans understand human equality, however, the situation is more serious. Unfortunately, it seems to us that however guileful many neoconservative opponents of equality are, they and many Americans simply do not adequately grasp what human equality requires. They fear and/or reject what they *imagine* equality to be, yet their imaginings lead them astray.

Genuine human equality is more complicated—"rich" is the better word—than either the supporters or opponents of American proprietary equality generally realize. It has two complementary aspects which must coexist: *respect for human dignity and material conditions adequate to support living dignified lives.* Neither moment in this dialectical, i.e., dynamic, conception of equality is sufficient in isolation from the other. Mere respect without the material conditions to support it is hollow; mere materialism without human dignity to underpin it is crass and destructive. How might we envision human equality? We think that a brief discussion of each of its elements will assist us to picture it.

Steven Lukes has analyzed the capacities which together comprise the uniqueness of being human. They provide a compelling basis for treating individuals as equals. The capacities are (1) relative autonomy, "the capacity of human beings to form intentions and purposes, to become aware of alternatives and choose between them, to acquire control over their own behaviour by becoming conscious of the forces determining it"; (2) creative activity and human relationships "the capacity to think thoughts, perform actions, develop involvements and engage in relationships to which they attach value...all [of which] require a space free and secure from external invasion or surveillance in order to flourish"; and (3) human excellence, "the capacity for human development."[45] Lukes summarizes the implications of his discussion of human capabilities as follows:

I have argued that these three characteristics of persons are at least part of the ground on which we accord them respect. What, then, does that respect consist in? The unsurprising answer is that, whatever else it involves, respecting them involves treating them as (actually or potentially) autonomous, as requiring a free and secure space for the pursuit of valued activities and relationships, and as capable of self-development. That answer has, given certain further assumptions, far-reaching social, economic and political implications, and points towards a society with substantially reduced inequalities, both of material and symbolic rewards and of political power.[46]

One aspect of human equality, then, entails recognition of the unique capacities which render us human. It entails, in other words, positing that we all are ontologically endowed with the capabilities to be autonomous, to be social, to be creative, and to pursue excellence. Of course, to what extent and in what manner these attributes work themselves out will differ from one individual to the next. The point is that *equal capacities give rise to the requirement of equal respect* which, in turn, entails a society

in which there were no barriers to reciprocal relations between relatively autonomous persons, who see each other and themselves as such, who are equally free from political control, social pressure and economic deprivation and insecurity to engage in valued pursuits, and who have equal access to the means of self-development. Such a society would not be marked by inequalities of power and privilege (which is not to say that a society without such inequalities would necessarily practise equal respect.)[47]

In this manner, one moment of the dialectic of human equality requires its complement; but just what is meant by equalities of power and privilege? Is not such equality merely a return to that leveling so properly criticized? Are we not calling for what we rejected above as simplistic? Our answer to both questions is no. The sort of material equality entailed by the principle of equal respect is proportional equality, a venerable concept tracing its origin to Aristotle's understanding of distributive justice.

In his *Nicomachean Ethics* Aristotle distinguished between two kinds of particular justice: corrective and distributive. Of the latter he wrote:

One form of partial justice and of what is just in this sense is found in the distribution of honors, of material goods, or of anything else that can be divided among those who have a share in the political system. For in these matters it is possible for a man to have a share equal or unequal to that of his neighbor.[48]

Aristotle argued that justice in the realm of distribution hinged upon equality between a person and his or her shares. A proportion must exist between what things a person receives and what that person deserves:

If the persons are not equal, their (just) shares will not be equal; but this is the source of quarrrels and recriminations, when equals have and are awarded unequal shares or unequals equal shares. The truth of this is further illustrated by the principle "To each according to his deserts." Everyone agrees that in distributions the just share must be given on the basis of what one deserves, though not everyone would name the same criterion of deserving. . . .[49]

Aristotle provides us with two crucial elements of an understanding of proportional equality: (1) a just distribution consists in a proportion between one's share(s) and one's merit; and (2) what "merit" consists in is the object of great controversy. Michael Walzer provides the third: equality requires a diversity of criteria for merit.[50] In this light, when we call for equality of wealth, income, power, and status, we are not advocating that such things should be distributed identically to all. Rather, we are advocating distribution of wealth, income, power, and status *in proportion to one's merit determined according to differing, appropriate criteria.* We agree with Walzer's statement, "A society in which any single distributive principle is dominant cannot be an egalitarian society. Equality requires a diversity of principles, which mirrors the diversity both of mankind and of social goods." Walzer concludes: "Our goal should be an end to tyranny, a society in which no man is master outside his sphere. That is the only society of equals worth having."[51] Democratic socialism diversifies the criteria for equality.

The reader would be justified at this point in asking how we imagine achieving the sort of society we and Walzer desire. Questions of this sort—What is to be done?—have a long and persistent lineage in political thought. Although there is no lack of answers to such questions, satisfactory answers are scarce; definitive ones, nonexistent. Nevertheless, we feel it is incumbent upon us to at least suggest what we consider to be one promising way to achieve genuine human equality in America. We do so bearing in mind the warnings in Kenneth Waltz's critique of efforts by behavioral scientists to end war:

They have fallen [into] the old rationalist fallacy, the identification of control with knowledge. They are assuming that once we know how to end war, we have solved the problem—that the problem is all one of knowing and not at all one of doing.... [Even] if the behavioral scientists can tell us what should be done to remove these causes, we still have a good bit more than half the battle to fight.[52]

Part of our program to achieve genuine human equality in America is contained in previous chapters. Affirmative action, the subject of section 2, and clear thinking, discussed in chapter 8, are both integral to any successful attempt at achieving genuine human equality. Perhaps we should say both are necessary but not sufficient conditions of such achievement. An additional condition, certainly necessary but not sufficient in that no social policies are panaceas, is a restructuring of production and ownership in the United States. Best and Connolly detail two specific proposals which we believe are prerequisites to reduced inequality:

    1. The system of production for private profit and private consumption (think of cars, individual houses, fashionable clothes) must increasingly be displaced by one of public ownership and the production of collective goods. Mass transit systems, health centers, recreation centers, schools are goods that can be made available to any citizen. To the extent that these collective goods become established in various spheres of life, the effective scope of inequality will be reduced.

    2. The system of work must be reformed so that, first, more jobs become fulfilling in their own right, and second, those necesary jobs that are not open to such reform become increasingly the part-time responsibility of all able-bodied members of the society, whatever their major occupations. These reforms will lessen the need for extreme pay differentials as an incentive to work, and they will have the important direct effect of reducing the extreme inequality of working conditions. Of course, these reforms will also require public ownership of the means of production; private owners will not accept meaningful reform voluntarily because...meaningful work

reform erodes the ability of private owners to control the productive system in their private interest. [53]

Best and Connolly's proposals speak to the substantive aspect of the question, What is to be done? The question's strategic implications remain to be addressed. Our suggestions with regard to strategy rest upon our conviction that so long as Americans continue to accept uncritically the assumptions of liberal-capitalism and behave accordingly, Hobson's choice—the choice between bigger government programs or "laissez faire" approaches to monopoly capital—will remain the only choice we have. Accordingly, we propose a twofold strategy aimed at changing peoples' values and changing society's institutions through educating and organizing.

Such a strategy, a dialectical, participatory set of means for creating a socialist—that is, egalitarian—society, has two primary thrusts, and operates on several fronts, through a diversity of vehicles. In general terms, this strategy takes as its keynote the perspective articulated well by Andre Gorz:

Socialism will not be achieved by a gradual reordering of the capitalist system, designed to rationalize its functioning and institutionalize class antagonisms. It will not emerge of its own accord out of the crises and imbalances of which capitalism can eliminate neither the causes nor the effects, but which it now knows how to prevent from becoming explosive, nor will it be born of a spontaneous uprising of the dissatisfied masses or through the anathematizing of social traitors and revisionists. It can be brought about only by deliberate, long-term action of which the beginning may be a scaled series of reform, but which, as it unfolds, must grow into a series of trials of strength...some won and others lost, but of which the outcome will be to mold and organize the socialist resolve and consciousness of the working classes. [54]

Socialist strategy must seek to impart critical skills and organizational strength to American workers; these are its two primary thrusts. By "critical skills" we mean the liberating ability to perceive those ideas, values, and attitudes one typically takes for granted in a disinterested light. To some extent, what we have in mind here is illustrated by the anthropologist's role as a student of cultures very different from his or her own. Just as the anthropologist is in the position to call into question aspects of a culture perceived as second nature by his or her subjects, the individual with critical skills probes typically intuitive ideas. The difference, of course, is that the anthropologist enjoys the advantages of being a stranger; advantages pertaining to heightened awareness and lessened intimacy and identification. Such critical skills will be learned only in the process of organizing to challenge and change the institutions to which culture generally conforms.

Socialist organizing must operate on several fronts and through a diversity of vehicles. This is required because the generality and pervasiveness of capitalist relations, not only throughout American society but internationally, demands a holistic, "totalist" strategy. We can better understand the reasons for such a strategy by realizing that it rests upon conceptual work done by several Marxists aimed at sophisticating the notions of "working class" and "factory" in Marxist analysis. As Harry Cleaver points out, such conceptualization begins from recognition that the "reproduction of the working class involves not only work in the factory but also work in the home and in the community of homes."[55] The resulting concept is that of the social factory. Cleaver explains:

The "factory" where the working class worked was the society as a whole, a social factory. The working class had to be redefined to include nonfactory workers. This theory provided a point of departure for understanding within a Marxist analysis not only the increasing number of struggles in the 1960s which involved students, women, and the unemployed in Italy, but also similar struggles elsewhere in Europe and the United States as well as those of peasants in the Third World...women like Mariarosa Dalla Costa developed both new theoretical emphases and new organizations.... They focused on the key role of the wage in hiding not only the unpaid part of the working day in the factory, but also the unpaid work outside it.... The identification of the leading role of the unwaged in the struggles of the 1960s in Italy, and the extension of the concept to the peasantry, provided a theoretical framework within which the struggles of American and European students and housewives, the unemployed, ethnic and racial minorities, and Third World peasants could all be grasped as moments of an international cycle of working-class struggle.[56]

It is in light of this sort of analysis that we argue that the struggle for genuine human equality must be multifarious. More specifically, we are convinced that greater equality will be won, if at all, in the homes, schools, churches, and offices of America as well as in the traditional arenas such as assembly lines, legislative halls, and court rooms. In order to carry out such comprehensive political struggles, a diversity of vehicles is required. To be sure, political parties are required to wage electoral battles on behalf of equality, and unions are needed to struggle on the working class—blue, white, and pink collar—front. Political parties and unions both must be modified from conventional American forms in that they "help the mass population not only gain an appreciation for the limitations, irrationalities, and injustice of the capitalist order, but to become transformed from a dominated, passive force to one that is self-confident, skilled, and practiced in socialist styles of life."[57] Additionally, vehicles such as women's groups, parents' groups, vocational and professional associations, church-based organizations, co-ops, and study groups must be enlisted in the struggle to fundamentally restructure the ways we think and act in relation to equality. In sum, a ground swell of change must be developed that will sweep aside what Michael Lewis termed the culture of inequality and the capitalist institutions which nurture it.

This strategy may strike the reader as hopelessly utopian. Even accepting the need to get beyond our present dilemma, epitomized by Hobson's choice, the strategy proposed here may seem to border on calling for a miracle. We acknowledge the imposing quality of what we think must be done. Still, in closing, we invite our readers to consider seriously the possibility of the "miraculous" in human affairs—the promise of politics. The odds against fundamental change are great, the force of inertia in human relations is large, continuity typically does predominate over change...*and yet,* as Hannah Arendt wrote in criticizing behavioral explanations of human aggressiveness, "The trouble is men can cheat."[58] We can cheat the odds, the inertia, the continuity, and all other varieties of reducing the human condition to its predictable, lawful components because we are also free—capable of acting and doing. Among Arendt's lasting contributions is her eloquent explication of the human political ability: to rise above conventional expectations, "the sheer capacity to begin, which animates and inspires all human activities and is the hidden source of production of all great and beautiful things."[59]

If we are going to achieve genuine human equality in America, we might begin by contemplating and practicing the sort of miraculous politics Arendt envisions in this passage:

Objectively, that is, seen from the outside and without taking into account that man is a beginning and a beginner, the chances that tomorrow will be like yesterday are always overwhelming. Not quite so overwhelming, to be sure, but very nearly so as the chances were that *no* earth would ever rise out of cosmic occurrences, that *no* life would develop out of inorganic processes, and that *no* man would emerge out of the evolution of animal life. The decisive difference between the "infinite improbabilities" on which the reality of our earthly life rests and the miraculous character inherent in those events which establish historical reality is that, in the realm of human affairs, we know the author of the "miracles." It is men who perform them—men who because they have received the twofold gift of freedom and action can establish a reality of their own.[60]

We are convinced that, in the final analysis, the constraints imposed by our present Hobson's choice with regard to equality are only as binding as we make them. We agree with Arendt that human choices are uniquely open-ended choices. Although we are not absolutely free from such restraining factors as the past, our physiology, and our social environment, we are able to act within such restraints to change the quality of our lives. That such actions are risky and difficult goes without saying (indeed, it seems to us that we are told about the problems associated with change all too often). Proprietary equality and monopoly capitalism are only "facts of life"—the "real world"—through default of action on our collective part to change them. We are stuck with existing realities only so long as we do not begin to fashion an alternative future.

NOTES

1. AMERICAN NOTIONS ABOUT EQUALITY

1. This definition is taken from Clifford Geertz, "Ideology as a Cultural System," in *The Interpretation of Cultures* (New York: Basic Books, 1973).

2. John Locke, *Two Treatises of Government,* ed. Peter Laslett (New York: Mentor Books, 1965), sec. 49, p. 343.

3. For example, in his controversial *Inventing America: Jefferson's Declaration of Independence* (Garden City, N.Y.: Doubleday, 1978), Garry Wills charts the influence of the Scottish Enlightenment upon Jefferson. Others have examined the republican tradition transmitted through such thinkers as Cicero, Augustine, Machiavelli, and Rousseau. See, for example, J.G.A. Pocock, *Politics, Language and Time* (New York: Atheneum, 1973), chs. 3 and 4. For a discussion of republican ideals in revolutionary America, see ch. 2 below.

4. Louis Hartz, *The Liberal Tradition in America* (New York: Harcourt, Brace & World, 1955), p. 3.

5. Thomas Hobbes, *Leviathan,* ed. W.G. Pogson Smith (London: Oxford University Press, 1962), p. 75.

6. It is important to point out that we understand the American political tradition to be Lockean and Hobbesian in metaphorical terms. This is to say that our political ideology incorporates analogously many of their concerns. In speaking of the Constitution as Hobbesian, for example, we refer to the underlying assumptions about power expressed in *Federalist* nos. 10, 47, 48, and 51. Because of the separation of powers and the adoption of a federal arrangement, the framers reached structural conclusions different from Hobbes's authoritarian government. Nevertheless, they shared to a large extent Hobbes's view of human nature and power. See Richard Hofstadter, *The American Political Tradition* (New York: Vintage Books, 1948), ch. 1.

7. Martin Diamond, "Democracy and the *Federalist,*" in *Intellectual History in America,* 2 vols., ed. Cushing Strout (New York: Harper & Row, 1968), 1:105.

8. C.B. Macpherson, *Possessive Individualism* (New York: Oxford University Press, 1964). It is important for the reader to understand our use of Macpherson's controversial interpretation of Hobbes and Locke. It is our view that his thesis reveals much about the substance of liberalism in America and the manner in which Hobbes and Locke influenced our dominant political ideology. While we are inclined to disagree with critics of Macpherson who variously contend that he misreads Hobbes and/or Locke, it is the utility of his interpretation for an understanding of American liberalism which concerns us. Even in the event that Macpherson is wrong about Hobbes's and Locke's theories functioning as ideologies for seventeenth-century bourgeois English capitalism, we maintain that his

view is highly instructive with regard to the tenor of liberalism in America. We invite the reader to peruse the critical literature on Macpherson's thesis and arrive at his or her own conclusions. Among the salient commentaries are: Isaiah Berlin, "Hobbes, Locke and Professor Macpherson," *Political Quarterly* 35 (1964): 444; George Lichtheim, "Possessive Individualism," *New Statesman* (London), Sept. 6, 1963, p. 287; Jacob Viner, "Possessive Individualism as Original Sin," *Canadian Journal of Economics and Political Science* 29 (Nov. 1963): 548, and Macpherson's rejoinder, ibid., p. 559; and Alan Ryan, "Locke and the Dictatorship of the Bourgeoisie," *Political Studies* 13 (1965): 219.

9. Macpherson, *Possessive Individualism,* p. 3.
10. Ibid., pp. 263-64.
11. Hobbes, *Leviathan,* p. 96.
12. Locke, *Two Treatises,* sec. 6, p. 311 (italics added).
13. Ibid., sec. 95, pp. 374-75.
14. Hobbes, *Leviathan,* p. 94.
15. Ibid., pp. 117-18.
16. Ibid., p. 95.
17. Jean-Jacques Rousseau, *Second Discourse,* ed. Roger D. Masters (New York: St. Martin's Press, 1964), pp. 94-96, 102-3, 107, 128-31.
18. Hobbes, *Leviathan,* pp. 96-97.
19. Locke, *Two Treatises,* sec. 4, p. 309.
20. Ibid., sec. 54, p. 346.
21. Chaim Perelman, *Justice* (New York: Random House, 1967), pp. 18-34.
22. J. L. Lucas, "Against Equality," in *Concepts in Social and Political Philosophy,* ed. Richard Flathman (New York: MacMillan, 1973), p. 349.
23. Locke, *Two Treatises,* sec. 87, p. 367.
24. Perelman, *Justice,* p. 7.
25. See the passages from Locke's writings cited by Macpherson in *Possessive Individualism,* pp. 223-25.
26. Macpherson, *Possessive Individualism,* pp. 246-47.
27. Murray Edelman, *The Symbolic Uses of Politics* (Urbana: University of Illinois Press, 1972), pp. 188-94.
28. Locke, *Two Treatises,* sec. 25, p. 327.
29. Ibid., sec. 27, p. 329.
30. Ibid., sec. 46-47, pp. 342-43 (italics added).
31. Ibid., sec. 50, pp. 343-44 (italics added).
32. Macpherson, *Possessive Individualism,* pp. 261-62.

2. PROPRIETARY EQUALITY IN AMERICA

1. Hector St. John de Crevecoeur quoted in Hannah Arendt, *On Revolution* (New York: Viking Press, 1965), p. 137.
2. Arendt, *On Revolution,* p. 115.
3. Gordon S. Wood, *The Creation of the American Republic, 1776-1787* (New York: W.W. Norton, 1972), p. 55.
4. Ibid., pp. 53-54.
5. This is Thorstein Veblen's term. See Veblen's *The Theory of the Leisure Class* (New York: Modern Library, 1934). Also see comments on Veblen and Michael Lewis below.
6. Arendt, *On Revolution,* p. 242.
7. Ibid., pp. 234-35.
8. Wood, *Creation of American Republic,* p. 608 (italics added).
9. Alexis de Tocqueville, *Democracy in America,* 2 vols., trans. Henry Reeve, ed. Phillips Bradley (New York: Vintage Books, 1945), 1:14.
10. Ibid., 1:117.
11. Ibid., 1:299, 300.
12. Ibid., 2:108 (italics added).

13. See Arendt, *On Revolution,* ch. 2.

14. Tocqueville, *Democracy in America,* 1:67.

15. Ibid., 2:104.

16. Ibid., 2:106.

17. John Stuart Mill, introduction to Tocqueville, *Democracy in America,* 2 vols., trans. Henry Reeve (New York: Schocken Books, 1961), 2:xlii.

18. Ibid., 2:xliii.

19. Ibid., 2:xlvii.

20. Tocqueville, *Democracy in America,* 2:144-45.

21. Ibid., 1:273.

22. Ibid., 1:274-75.

23. For example, see Richard Hofstadter, *Anti-Intellectualism in American Life* (New York: Vintage Books, 1963).

24. Barry Susman, "Party Workers Poles Apart," *Washington Post,* Sept. 27, 1976.

25. Marvin Meyers, *The Jacksonian Persuasion: Politics and Beliefs* (New York: Vintage Books, 1957), pp. 55-56.

26. Joseph L. Blau, ed., *Social Theories of Jacksonian Democracy* (Indianapolis: Bobbs-Merrill, 1954), p. 374.

27. William Leggett, "Objects of the *Evening Post,*" in ibid., pp. 72-73.

28. Dartmouth College was granted a charter by the English crown in 1769 that created a board of trustees who were empowered to govern the affairs of the new college. When the founder and first president of the college died, his son, John Wheelock, become president. However, Wheelock was removed from the presidency by the board of trustees after numerous unpleasant conflicts. The two political parties in the state were also drawn into the controversy, the Federalists supporting the trustees while the Republicans sided with Wheelock. In 1816 the Republican majority in the state legislature enacted three laws that amended the original charter and provided for a new governing body for the institution, whose name was changed to Dartmouth University. The old trustees refused to be governed by the new law and continued to run the college. The new 'state' trustees appointed by the governor 'removed' the old trustees and reelected Wheelock to the presidency. The old board of trustees contended that the 1816 legislation impaired the obligation of contracts contained in the original charter of 1769 and sued in the state courts to recover possession of the college charter, records, seal, and accounts from Woodward, the secretary of the new board. The state courts ruled against the college. The old trustees then took the case to the Supreme Court on a writ of error.

29. Daniel Henshaw, "The Dartmouth College Case," in Blau, *Social Theories of Jacksonian Democracy,* p. 172 (italics added).

30. Theodore Sedgwick, Jr., "What Is a Monopoly," in ibid., p. 234. It is important to point out the continuity in Democratic thought and action with regard to Sedgwick's remark, "They are the best friends of property and of men of property who would abolish every unequal and unrighteous means of acquiring it." From Woodrow Wilson's progressivism, through Franklin D. Roosevelt's New Deal, up until the welfare state liberalism epitomized by Lyndon Johnson, Hubert Humphrey, and Ted Kennedy, Democrats have sought to use the state to perpetuate capitalism by mollifying its crises and compensating for its worst injustices.

31. James Willard Hurst, *Law and the Conditions of Freedom in the Nineteenth-Century United States* (Madison: University of Wisconsin Press, 1956), pp. 6-7.

32. Ibid., p. 16 (italics added).

33. This is Ray Ginger's term. See his *The Age of Excess* (New York: Macmillan, 1971).

34. See Horatio Alger, *Ragged Dick and Mark, the Match Boy* (New York: Collier Books, 1962).

35. Robert G. McCloskey, *American Conservatism in the Age of Enterprise, 1865-1910* (New York: Harper & Row, 1964), p. 20.

36. Thomas Hobbes, *Leviathan,* ed. Michael Oakeshott (New York: Collier Books, 1962), p. 81.

37. Ginger, *Age of Excess,* p. 19.
38. McCloskey, *American Conservatism,* p. 42.
39. Ibid., p. 43.
40. Ibid., p. 47.
41. Ibid., pp. 49, 50.
42. Richard Hofstadter, *Social Darwinism in American Thought,* rev. ed. (Boston: Beacon Press, 1955), p. 56.
43. McCloskey, *American Conservatism,* pp. 86-87.
44. Arnold M. Paul, *Conservative Crisis and the Rule of Law* (New York: Harper & Row, 1969).
45. Matthew Josephson, *The Robber Barons* (New York: Harcourt, Brace & World, 1962), p. 18.
46. McCloskey, *American Conservatism,* p. 147.
47. Daniel Drew, *The Book of Daniel Drew* (New York: Frontier Press, 1969), pp. 18-19.
48. Ibid., pp. 144-45.
49. Andrew Carnegie, *Autobiography* (Boston: Houghton Mifflin, 1920). These are terms used to head sections of this book.
50. Ibid., p. 338.
51. Andrew Carnegie, *Problems of To-day* (New York: Doubleday, Page, 1909), pp. 152-53.
52. Ibid., pp. 174-76.
53. See Michael Lewis, *The Culture of Inequality* (Amherst, Mass.: University of Massachusetts Press, 1978), part 1.
54. Ibid., p. 8.
55. Ibid., pp. 14-19.
56. Ibid. p. 12.
57. For analyses of both these positions, see Frances Fox Piven and Richard A. Cloward, *Regulating the Poor* (New York: Vintage Books, 1972) and William Ryan, *Blaming the Victim* (New York: Vintage Books, 1976).
58. Lewis, *Culture of Inequality,* pp. 11-12.
59. Ibid., p. 195.

3. AFFIRMATIVE ACTION

1. Robert Nozick, *Anarchy, State, and Utopia* (New York: Basic Books, 1974).
2. Daniel Bell, "On Meritocracy and Equality," *Public Interest* 39 (Fall, 1972): 29-68.
3. John Rawls, *A Theory of Justice* (Cambridge: Harvard University Press, 1971).
4. Martin Luther King, cited in Leo Huberman and Paul Sweezy, *Introduction of Socialism* (New York: Monthly Review Press, 1968), p. 17.
5. Executive Order 8802, 8 *Federal Register* 1815 (1943).
6. President Lyndon B. Johnson, address to graduating class, Howard University, June 4, 1965, cited in Thomas Dye, *Understanding Public Policy,* 2nd ed. (Englewood Cliffs, N.J.: Prentice-Hall, 1975), p. 62.
7. Executive Order 11246 was amended to include sex (along with race, creed, color, and national origin) when President Johnson issued Executive Order 11375 on Oct. 13, 1967.
8. The following account of the Philadelphia Plan is based in part on James Jones, "The Bugaboo of Employment Quotas," *Wisconsin Law Review* (1970): 344-73; and James Hardgrove, "The Philadelphia Plan," *Notre Dame Lawyer* 65 (1970): 681-82.
9. Robert Schuwerk, "The Philadelphia Plan: A Study in the Dynamics of Executive Power," *University of Chicago Law Review* 39 (1971-72): 723-60.
10. U.S. Equal Employment Opportunity Commission, *Affirmative Action and Equal Employment* 1 (Washington, D.C.: 1974): 6.
11. Chief Justice Warren Burger quoted in ibid., p. 6.

4. *BAKKE* AND EDUCATIONAL OPPORTUNITY

1. Additionally, most institutions of higher education receive federal grants and are therefore bound by Title VI of the 1964 Civil Rights Act (42 U.S.C., sec. 200d *et seq.*), which prohibits discrimination in the operation of federally assisted programs. Regulations issued by the Department of Health and Human Services pursuant to Title VI authorize affirmative action to correct conditions that limit the participation of minorities even in the absence of prior discrimination. See 45 C.F.R. 80, 3(b)(6)(ii). U.S. Civil Rights Commission, *Statement on Affirmative Action,* p. 8.

2. For example, an earned doctorate is usually the minimal qualification for an entry-level teaching position in an academic department of a college or university; beyond that floor, teaching experience and publications may differentiate candidates.

3. These distinctions regarding types of reverse discrimination are sometimes reduced to the two categories of "weak" and "strong" reverse discrimination. Preferring unqualified women or minorities to qualified white men would constitute strong reverse discrimination, while the other two types mentioned in the text would fall under the heading of weak reverse discrimination. See Alan Goldman, "Affirmative Action," *Philosophy and Public Affairs* 5 (Winter, 1976): 178.

4. *Higher Education Guidelines: Executive Order 11246* (Washington, D.C.: Office of Civil Rights, Department of Health, Education and Welfare, October 1972), pp. 4, 8. See also the Dec., 1974, "Memorandum to College and University Presidents" written by Peter Holmes, then director of the Office of Civil Rights.

5. 42 U.S.C. sec. 2000d.

6. Brennan's opinion in the *Bakke* case stresses this point heavily. It was concern with southern hospitals, for example, which received federal funds yet refused to admit blacks, that prompted the adoption of Title VI.

7. Since the equal protection clause reads that "no state shall...," the Court has held that where official state policy is not involved to some degree, a plaintiff has no cause of action. Federal policy is also included in the concept, usually under the aegis of the Fifth Amendment guarantee of due process.

5. *WEBER* AND EMPLOYMENT OPPORTUNITY

1. Jo Freeman, *The Politics of Women's Liberation* (New York: McKay, 1975), p. 175.

2. Ibid., pp. 53-54, 178.

3. Ibid., p. 54.

4. Interview with Raymond Lorentz, voluntary programs office, New York office of the U.S. Equal Employment Opportunity Commission, Feb. 15, 1976.

5. The Office of Federal Contract Compliance under the Department of Labor interprets the executive orders and issues guidelines, directives, and regulations for complying with the executive orders. The OFCC has delegated authority to enforce Revised Order No. 4 in relation to universities to the Civil Rights Division of the Department of Health and Human Services, which first issued guidelines for affirmative action in universities in October, 1972.

6. Robert Schuwerk, "The Philadelphia Plan: A Study in the Dynamics of Executive Power," *University of Chicago Law Review* 39 (1971-72): 723-60.

7. See ch. 3 above for a discussion of the Philadelphia Plan.

8. See ch. 3 above for a discussion of this process of congressional scrutiny.

9. There are numerous attempts to differentiate goals from quotas. One approach contrasts goals and quotas by *purpose* (benign or inclusive versus invidious or exclusive) and by *bindingness* (loose versus fixed, flexible versus rigid, general versus specific). In this view, a goal is a flexible target which employers must make (demonstrable) good faith efforts to meet but which must not be satisfied at the sacrifice of merit, standards, and qualifications. By contrast, a quota is any fixed numerical requirement which must be met

within a certain time period, regardless of whether the applicant selected is qualified for the position. The Carnegie Council distinguishes a quota and a goal as follows:

Quota	Goal
An assigned share	An intention
A proportional result	An aim
A fixed division of numbers	A purpose
Must be met	Try to meet
Precise—no variation above or below	Subject to variation depending on circumstances
Rigid	
Permanent	Subject to change over time
	Can be abandoned when no longer needed

Source: Carnegie Council on Policy Studies in Higher Education, *Selective Admissions in Higher Education* (San Francisco: Jossey-Bass, 1977), n. 9, p. 15. It should be noted that any two-track system applying different standards of admission or hiring will inevitably involve a quota, since a fixed number of seats are designated and restricted to certain groups. Actually such a two-tiered approach will involve a minimal and a maximal quota (minimal for minorities and maximal for nonminorities).

10. See ch. 4 above. Some define as reverse discrimination any policy which takes factors of race, sex, religion, color, or national origin into account; in this view, the only way to avoid reverse discrimination is to adopt a strictly neutral, colorblind approach. See, for example, Barbara Lorch, "Reverse Discrimination in Hiring in Sociology Departments: A Preliminary Report," *American Sociologist* 8 (Aug., 1973): 116-20. Others distinguish weak from strong types of reverse discrimination: weak reverse discrimination is giving preference to minority candidates who are as well qualified as other candidates, while strong reverse discrimination occurs in giving preference to minority candidates who are less qualified than others. See Alan Goldman, "Affirmative Action," *Philosophy and Public Affairs* 5 (Winter, 1976): 178.

11. See, for example, "Minority Hiring Said To Hurt Colleges," *New York Times,* June 28, 1974, p. 1; and Midge Decter, "On Affirmative Action and Lost Respect, *New York Times,* July 6, 1980, Op-Ed page.

12. Goldman, "Affirmative Action," questions whether affirmative action programs in fact function to encourage reverse discrimination; without citing any empirical evidence to support his claim, he concludes that they do. In "Compensatory Justice: The Question of Costs," *Political Theory* 7 (May, 1979), Robert Amdur simply assumes that white males are being discriminated against and goes on to argue that they should not bear an unfair share of the cost of compensating minorities and women for past discrimination.

13. *New York Times,* Nov. 10, 1974, sec. 3, pp. 1-2.

14. Bernice Sandler, "A Little Help from Our Government: WEAL and Contract Compliance," in *Academic Women on the Move,* ed. Alice Rossi and Anne Calderwood (New York: Russell Sage Foundation, 1973), pp. 440-41.

15. Lorch, "Reverse Discrimination," pp. 116-20.

16. According to Lorch, her respondents explained this discrepancy as being "caused by several varied circumstances. In some cases the coercion was resisted; in others the woman or minority group members turned down the offer of the department, and it then turned to its best candidate, who as an Anglo male; in some cases the best candidate for the job was a woman or a minority group member; in some cases women and minority candidates for the position could not be solicited because of the short supply of such candidates." Ibid., p. 120.

17. Ibid., p. 119 (italics in original).

18. In fairness to Lorch, her article preceded by five years the Supreme Court's decision in the *Bakke* case.

19. The majority opinion, written by Justice Brennan, was joined by Associate Justices Stewart, White, Marshall, and Blackmun, who also filed a concurring opinion. Chief Justice Burger and Associate Justice Rehnquist both filed strong dissenting opinions. Justice John Paul Stevens did not take part in the case because he had done legal work for Kaiser when he was in private practice. Justice Lewis Powell missed oral argument because of illness and chose not to take part in the decision.

20. The particular congressional statute was the Public Works Employment Act of 1977. According to this law, a minority business enterprise was defined as a company in which blacks, Hispanic-Americans, oriental Americans, Eskimos, American Indians, or Aleuts controlled at least 50 percent interest. *New York Times,* July 3, 1980, p. D15.
21. Chief Justice Warren Burger wrote a plurality opinion in which Justices White and Powell joined. Justice Powell also filed a concurring opinion. Justice Marshall filed an opinion concurring in the judgment in which Justices Brennan and Blackmun joined. Justice Stewart wrote a dissent in which Justice Rehnquist joined. Justice Stevens wrote a separate dissent.
22. *New York Times,* July 4, 1980, p. A12.

6. JUSTIFYING AFFIRMATIVE ACTION

1. The United States Civil Rights Commission in its "Statement on Affirmative Action," published October, 1977, defines affirmative action as "a term that in a broad sense encompasses any measure, beyond simple termination of discriminatory practice, adopted to correct or compensate for past or present discrimination or to prevent discrimination from recurring in the future" (p. 2).
2. See John H. Schaar, "Equality of Opportunity, and Beyond," in *Equality: Nomos IX,* ed. J.R. Pennock and J.W. Chapman (New York: Atherton, 1967), p. 230.
3. John Charvet, "The Idea of Equality as a Substantive Principle of Society," *Political Studies,* 1969, pp. 1-13.
4. This position is argued by Irving Kristol, Nathan Glazer, Daniel Bell, and other neoconservatives. See, for example, Samuel Huntington, "The Democratic Distemper," in *The American Commonwealth — 1976,* ed. Nathan Glazer and Daniel P. Moynihan (New York: Basic Books, 1976), pp. 9-38; and Daniel Bell, "Meritocracy," in his *The Coming of Post-Industrial Society* (New York: Basic Books, 1973), pp. 408-55.
5. Schaar, "Equality of Opportunity," pp. 231-33.
6. Ibid., p. 229.
7. President Lyndon B. Johnson, address to graduating class, Howard University, June 4, 1965, cited in Thomas Dye, *Understanding Public Policy,* 2d ed. (Englewood Cliffs, N.J.: Prentice-Hall, 1975), p. 62.
8. Earl Rabb, "Quotas by Any Other Name," *Commentary,* Jan., 1972, p. 4.
9. J.L. Lucas, "Against Equality," in *Concepts in Social and Political Philosophy,* ed. Richard Flathman (New York: Macmillan, 1973), p. 350.
10. James W. Nickel, "Preferential Policies in Hiring and Admissions: A Jurisprudential Approach," *Columbia Law Review,* April, 1975, p. 6.
11. Thomas Nagel, "Equal Treatment and Compensatory Discrimination," *Philosophy and Public Affairs* 2 (Summer, 1973): 361.
12. Ibid., p. 362.
13. This argument is made most frequently and forcefully by Thomas Sowell. See his "The Plight of Black Students in the United States," *Daedalus,* Spring, 1974, p. 187; also his "A Black 'Conservative' Dissents," *New York Times Magazine,* Aug. 8, 1976, p. 14.
14. See, for example, Richard Rodriguez, "A Mexican-American Protests That Affirmative Action Is Unfair to Minorities," *Politicks and Other Human Interests,* Dec. 6, 1977, pp. 13-14.
15. George Sher, "Justifying Reverse Discrimination in Employment," *Philosophy and Public Affairs* 4 (Winter, 1975): 159-60.
16. John Rawls, *A Theory of Justice* (Cambridge: Harvard University Press, 1971), p. 28.
17. Sher, "Justifying Reverse Discrimination," p. 160, note 1 (emphasis in original).
18. Amitai Etzioni, "Making Up for Past Injustice: How *Bakke* Could Backfire," *Psychology Today,* Aug., 1977, p. 18.
19. Hugo Bedau, "Compensatory Justice: Sorts of Cases and Principles," paper delivered at the World Congress on Philosophy of Law and Social Philosophy, Madrid, Spain, Sept. 7-12, 1973, p. 9.

20. Aristotle, *Nicomachean Ethics,* trans. J.A.K. Thomson (London: Penguin Books, 1955), bk. 5, pp. 144-45.

21. Ibid.

22. See, for example, Donal E.J. MacNamara and John J. Sullivan, "Making the Victim Whole," *Urban Review* 6 (1973): 21-25. Here the focus is not on the concept of offender-restitution (presumably the offender is "paying his debt to society" by serving time in prison). Rather this article concerns victim compensation by the state which presumably failed (through defective police protection) to protect the victim adequately. Victim compensation laws have been enacted by the states of New York and California (1965), Hawaii (1967), Massachusetts and Maryland (1968), and New Jersey (1971).

23. In many cases of legal compensation for injuries done or losses suffered, the damages awarded do not restore a person to the *status quo ante,* but compensate with the goal of restoring the person to the condition he would have been in had the damage not occurred. See Nickel, "Preferential Policies," pp. 3-4, and MacNamara and Sullivan, "Making the Victim Whole," p. 23.

24. Bedau, "Compensatory Justice," pp. 3-4.

25. B.I. Bittker, *The Case for Black Reparations* (New York: Random House, 1973).

26. Ibid., pp. 87-127.

27. Hana Stranska, "Compensatory Comparisons," *New York Times Magazine,* Dec. 1, 1974, p. 14.

28. H.A. Deane, "Justice—Compensatory and Distributive," 1974 Columbia University (Typescript), pp. 13-14.

29. Solicitor General, Department of Justice, Brief for the United States as amicus curiae, *Regents of the University of California* v. *Bakke,* no. 76-811, at 56.

30. Earl Rabb, letter to the editor, *Commentary,* May, 1972, p. 30.

31. This argument is made most clearly by Deane in "Justice—Compensatory and Distributive." He argues there that "nothing but confusion is achieved by talking about these claims as though they were demands for the application of the principles of corrective justice" (p. 8).

32. For a recent review of pertinent data, see Andrew Hacker, "Creating American Inequality," *New York Review of Books* 27 (Mar. 20, 1980): 20-28.

33. Sher, "Justifying Reverse Discrimination," p. 163.

34. Nickel, "Preferential Policies," p. 3.

35. We are indebted to Tema Javerbaum, "'Grappling' with the *Bakke* Case: Some Questions and Justifications," Rutgers University, 1978 (typescript), for bringing this to our attention.

36. The reader should be alerted to the fact that, in the present context, the term "compensate" does not necessarily mean recompensing a person for *past* injuries. Nickel notes that, although programs using preferential policies to increase educational and employment opportunities for minorities "are often called *compensatory,* they are not necessarily designed to meet the requirements of compensatory justice by providing compensation for *past* wrongs. To compensate is merely to counterbalance, and the counterbalancing of disadvantages can be done for reasons other than those of compensatory justice." Nickel, "Preferential Policies," p. 2.

37. The Carnegie Council on Policy Studies in Higher Education recommends the following in this connection: "No student should be admitted who cannot meet the general academic standards set for all students. These standards should be set, through assessment of prior grades and test scores and personal qualifications, at the minimum level at which there is a reasonable chance of success in completing the course work without reduction in academic or professional standards. Race, other minority status, or sex is clearly not a consideration here. One source of help in determining this level is to look at the level of, say, 10 years ago when competition for admission was less intense but competent graduates and practitioners were being trained." Carnegie Council, *Selective Admissions,* pp. 14-15.

38. Benjamin Ringer, "Affirmative Action, Quotas and Meritocracy," *Society* (Jan.-Feb., 1976), p. 25.

7. EVALUATING AFFIRMATIVE ACTION

1. David Rosenbaum, "Working Women Still Seek Man-Sized Wages," *New York Times,* July 27, 1980, p. E3.

2. Andrew Hacker, "Creating American Inequality," *The New York Review of Books* 27 (March 20, 1980): 22.

3. Ibid., p. 23.

4. Rosenbaum, "Working Women Seek Wages"; and Jerry Flint, "Washington Plans Affirmative Action Push in '79," *New York Times,* Dec. 24, 1978, pp. F1-F2.

5. The best account of this case is *Equal Employment and the AT&T Case,* ed. Phyllis A. Wallace (Cambridge, Mass.: MIT Press, 1976).

6. The United States Judicial Conference is similar to a board of directors for the federal court system. It is headed by Chief Justice Warren F. Burger and is composed of 25 other high-ranking federal judges.

7. *New York Times,* Mar. 7, 1980, p. B7.

8. *New York Times,* Jan. 10, 1981, p. 16.

9. The PACE exam was a primary means of screening applicants for a large number of federal white-collar jobs, including customs inspectors, tax examiners, and social security adjusters.

10. *New York Times,* Oct. 1, 1980, p. A18.

11. *New York Times,* Nov. 2, 1980, p. 33.

12. For example, in response to inquiries from institutions and groups about the distinction between goals and quotas, the Justice and Labor Departments, the EEOC, and the Civil Service Commission signed in March, 1973, a four-agency agreement stating, by way of clarification, that quotas were illegal. See Marylin Bender, "Job Discrimination, Ten Years after the Ban," *New York Times,* Nov. 10, 1974, sec. 3, pp. 1, 5.

13. *New York Times,* Jan. 25, 1979, pp. A1, A13.

14. Ibid., p. A1.

15. *New York Times,* May 16, 1979, p. D18.

16. In 1973, Sears, a major employer of women, had become the target of an investigation by the EEOC. In April, 1977, the commission decided to press ahead with charges against Sears. Between 1977 and 1979, when the suit was filed, the company and the commission had been engaged in the conciliation negotiations that are required before any legal action is taken by the government.

17. *New York Times,* May 16, 1979, p. D18.

18. Under the LIFO principle ("Last in, first out") operative with respect to seniority positions, those most recently hired would be the first to lose their jobs in the event of cutbacks in the work force.

19. *New York Times,* Aug. 12, 1980, p. B6.

8. CONCEPTUAL PREMISES

1. David Hume, *An Inquiry into the Principles of Morals,* ed. C.W. Hendel (New York: Bobbs-Merrill, 1957).

2. John Wilson, *Equality* (New York: Harcourt, Brace & World, 1966), pp. 40-41. Wilson proceeds to demolish this distinction by demonstrating that what we perceive as natural is necessarily an artifact of human language.

3. Ibid., pp. 42-51.

4. Ibid., p. 64.

5. Jean Jacques Rousseau, *The First and Second Discourses,* ed. R.D. Masters (New York: St. Martins, 1964).

6. John Rawls, *A Theory of Justice* (Cambridge: Harvard University Press, 1971), p. 102.

7. John Plamenatz, "Diversity of Rights and Kinds of Equality," in *Equality: Nomos IX,* ed. J.R. Pennock and J.W. Chapman (New York: Atherton, 1967), p. 79. Hence to

establish true equality would imply abolishing the division of labor. This idea is at the heart of the orthodox Marxist precept that inequality is the product of capitalist division of labor, and that true equality will only be possible once that division of labor is overcome. See Marx's famous "hunt in the morning, fish in the after noon..." statement in *The German Ideology,* ed. C.J. Arthur (New York: International Publishers, 1970), p. 53.

8. In the Manifesto of the Equals, Babeuf and Merechal were willing to maintain that the only permissible differences should be those of age and sex. See V. Advielle, *Histoire de Gracchus Babeuf et de Babouvisme* (Paris: 1884), cited in Sanford Lakoff, *Equality in Political Philosophy* (Cambridge: Harvard University Press, 1964), pp. 112-25. The more widely accepted position among egalitarians is the one which tries to reconcile equality with the widest possible acceptance of human differences. This view is expressed in ch. 9 of this book and by R.H. Tawney, *Equality* (New York: Capricorn, 1961, originally published 1931).

9. See Max Weber, *The Theory of Social and Economic Organization,* trans. A.M. Henderson and Talcott Parsons (New York: Macmillan, 1964), pp. 152-53.

10. See Robert Dahl, *Modern Political Analysis,* 3d ed. (Englewood Cliffs, N.J.: Prentice-Hall, 1976); and Dahl, *Polyarchy* (New Haven: Yale University Press, 1971).

11. See bibliography for this literature.

12. This is the advantage of the position taken by Stanley Benn that equality consists in the equal consideration of interests. See S.I. Benn, "Equality and Equal Consideration of Interests," in Pennock and Chapman, *Equality,* pp. 61-78.

13. Hugo Bedau, "Egalitarianism and the Idea of Equality," in Pennock and Chapman, *Equality,* pp. 3-27.

14. Any consideration of justice and its relation to equality brings one back to Aristotle. See *The Politics,* ed. and trans. Sir Ernest Barker (New York: Oxford University Press, 1962); and *Nicomachean Ethics,* trans. Martin Oswald (Indianapolis: Bobbs-Merrill, 1962).

15. Wilson, *Equality,* pp. 114-21.

16. Rejection of egalitarianism on grounds of economic efficiency has been almost as pervasive in existing socialist systems as in capitalism. Doctrinal legitimacy for such "socialist" rejections is typically traced to Marx's statements in his *Critique of the Gotha Program.* See Karl Marx, *Critique of the Gotha Program,* ed. C.P. Dutt (New York: International Publishers, 1966), pp. 9-11.

17. Bedau, "Egalitariansim," pp. 18-19.

18. See Rawls's critique of utilitariansim on this point, *Theory of Justice,* pp. 22-27. For an excellent discussion of aggregative and distributive principles in political and economic theory, see Brian Barry, *Political Argument* (London: Routledge & Kegan Paul, 1965), pp. 43-47.

19. Marx, *Critique on the Gotha Program,* pp. 9-10.

20. Bedau, "Egalitarianism," pp. 9-10. In Bedau's original example, one person wanted a guitar and the other a banjo. We have substituted a piano to magnify the differences in order to make a slightly different point than that for which Bedau originally used the example.

21. The distinction between want regarding principles and ideal regarding principles strikes us as one of the most useful concepts in political theory. It is presented excellently in Barry, *Political Argument,* pp. 38-43.

22. S.I. Benn and R.S. Peters, *Principles of Political Thought,* (New York: Free Press, 1965), p. 136.

23. George Sher, "Justifying Reverse Discrimination in Employment," in *Equality and Preferential Treatment,* ed. Marshall Cohen and Thomas Scanlon (Princeton: Princeton University Press, 1977), p. 50.

24. Ronald Dworkin, "DeFunis v. Sweatt," in Cohen and Scanlon, *Equality,* p. 67.

9. POLITICAL ECONOMY OF EQUALITY

1. The terms "reform liberals" and "neoconservatives" are intended to represent political tendencies, especially with reference to equality, instead of specific individuals. Nevertheless, it may be useful to say that the reform liberal position is exemplified by the so-called left wing of the Democratic Party, groups such as the Americans for Democratic Action, and people such as the late Lyndon B. Johnson, Hubert H. Humphrey, and Ted Kennedy. The neoconservative stance is articulated in *Public Interest* and *Commentary,* and exemplified by the views of such people as Irving Kristol, Daniel Bell, Robert Nisbet, Daniel Patrick Moynihan, and Nathan Glazer.

2. Thomas Hobson was a liveryman, inventor, and benefactor of the city of Cambridge, England. In the words of Webster's *New International Dictionary* (2d ed.): "Hobson's choice is a choice without an alternative; the thing offered or nothing;—so-called in allusion to the practice of Thomas Hobson (d. 1631), at Cambridge, England, who let horses, and required every customer to take the horse which stood nearest the door."

3. Paul Blumberg, *Inequality in an Age of Decline* (New York: Oxford University Press, 1980), p. 7.

4. Howard Sherman, *Radical Political Economy: Capitalism and Socialism from a Marxist-Humanist Perspective* (New York: Basic Books, 1972), p. 3.

5. Ibid., p. 6.

6. Michael Best and William Connolly, *The Politicized Economy* (Lexington, Mass.: D.C. Heath, 1976), pp. xiv-xv.

7. Thorstein Veblen, *The Theory of the Leisure Class* (New York: Modern Library, 1934), p. 30.

8. Andrew Hacker, "Creating American Inequality," *New York Review of Books* 27 (Mar. 20, 1980): 27-28.

9. Edward S. Greenberg, *Serving the Few: Corporate Capitalism and the Bias of Government Policy* (New York: Wiley, 1974) p. 88.

10. Best and Connolly, *Politicized Economy,* p. 96.

11. Karl Marx, *Critique of the Gotha Program,* ed. C.P. Dutt (New York: International Publishers, 1966). pp. 10-11.

12. Frank Ackerman and Andrew Zimbalist, "Capitalism and Inequality in the United States," in *The Capitalist System,* ed. Richard Edwards, Michael Reich, and Thomas Weisskopf, 2d ed. (Englewood Cliffs, N.J.: Prentice-Hall, 1978), pp. 306-7.

13. For our understanding of the term "working class" see Harry Cleaver, *Reading Capital Politically* (Austin: University of Texas Press, 1979).

14. By this we do not mean that all who must labor suffer exactly the same, but that all workers are in the same situation of dependency and, hence, vulnerability.

15. Karl Marx, *Capital,* 3 vols., trans. Samuel Moore and Edward Aveling, ed. Frederick Engels (New York: International Publishers, 1967), 1:35.

16. Cleaver, *Reading Capital Politically,* p. 74.

17. Ibid., pp. 72-73.

18. Christopher Jencks et al., *Inequality: A Reassessment of the Effect of Family and Schooling in America* (New York: Harper & Row, 1973), p. 265.

19. Michael Harrington, *Socialism* (New York: Bantam Books, 1973), pp. 338-39.

20. Harrington, *Twilight of Capitalism* (New York: Simon & Schuster, 1976), p. 307.

21. Greenberg, *Serving the Few,* pp. 155-56.

22. Greenberg, *The American Political System: A Radical Approach* (Cambridge: Winthrop, 1977), p. 129.

23. For a brilliant discussion of the differences between natural and artificial inequalities— inequalities based upon human differences and inequalities based upon income—see Michael Walzer, "In Defense of Equality," in *The New Conservatives,* ed. Lewis Coser and Irving Howe (New York: New American Library, 1973).

24. Barry Weisberg, *Beyond Repair: The Ecology of Capitalism* (Boston: Beacon, 1971), p. 73 (emphasis added).

25. Andre Gorz, *Ecology as Politics,* trans. Patsy Vigderman and Jonathan Cloud (Boston: South End Press, 1980), pp. 32-34.
26. Walter Dean Burnham, "American Politics in the 1980s," *Dissent,* Spring, 1980, p. 159.
27. Robert Dahl, "The Concept of Power," in *Political Power: A Reader in Theory and Research,* ed. Roderick Bell, David V. Edwards, and R. Harrison Wagner (New York: Free Press, 1969).
28. See C. Wright Mills, *The Sociological Imagination* (New York: Oxford University Press, 1959), ch. 10.
29. Peter Steinfels, *The Neoconservatives,* (New York: Simon & Schuster, 1979), p. 51.
30. Edwards, Reich, and Weisskopf, *Capitalist System,* p. 117.
31. Michael Reagan, *The Managed Economy,* (New York: Oxford University Press, 1963), p. 18.
32. Daniel Bell, *The Coming of Post-Industrial Society,* cited in Harrington, *Twilight of Capitalism,* p. 221.
33. Ibid.
34. Reagan, *Managed Economy,* p. 142.
35. Roosevelt's term is cited in Leo Huberman and Paul M. Sweezy, *Introduction to Socialism* (New York: Monthly Review, 1968), p. 45. The phrase is "Necessitous men are not free men," and it was spoken in Roosevelt's State of the Union message to Congress, January 11, 1944.
36. Gorz, *Strategy for Labor,* trans. Martin A. Nicolaus and Victoria Ortiz (Boston: Beacon Press, 1964), pp. 66-67.
37. See Daniel Bell, "Meritocracy and Equality," *Public Interest,* Fall, 1972.
38. Best and Connolly, *Politicized Economy,* pp. 84-85.
39. The following summary is derived from Best and Connolly, *Politicized Economy,* pp. 87-90. Cf. K. Davis and W. Moore, "Some Principles of Stratification,"in *Class, Status and Power,* ed. R. Bendix and S.M. Lipset, 2d ed. (London: Routledge, 1967).
40. Herbert Gans, "The Uses of Poverty: The Poor Pay All," *Social Policy* 2 (July-August, 1971).
41. *U.S. News & World Report,* Aug. 14, 1971, pp. 23-25. More recent statistics bear out this same argument; see Richard C. Edwards, "Who Fares Well in the Welfare State?" in Edwards, Reich, and Weiskopf, *Capitalist System,* pp. 307-15.
42. *U.S. News,* p. 25.
43. John Schaar, "Equality of Opportunity, and Beyond,"in *Equality: Nomos IX,* ed. J.R. Pennock and J.W. Chapman (New York: Atherton, 1967), pp. 247-48.
44. "Neoconservative fears" is Steinfels's phrase and this is his listing. See *The Neoconservatives,* ch. 9.
45. Steven Lukes, "Socialism and Equality," in *The Socialist Idea: A Reappraisal,* ed. Leszek Kolakowski and Stuart Hampshire (London: Quartet Books, 1977), pp. 77-78.
46. Ibid., p. 78.,
47. Ibid., p. 82.
48. Aristotle, *Nicomachean Ethics,* trans. Martin Ostwald (Indianapolis: Bobbs-Merrill, 1962), bk. 5., sec. 30. p. 117.
49. Ibid., bk. 5., sec. 20-25, pp. 118-19.
50. See Walzer, "In Defense of Equality."
51. Ibid., pp. 112, 114.
52. Kenneth N. Waltz, *Man, the State and War* (New York: Columbia University Press, 1954), p. 59.
53. Best and Connolly, *Politicized Economy,* p. 98.
54. Gorz, *Socialism and Revolution* (New York: Doubleday, 1973), p. 136.
55. Cleaver, *Reading Capital Politically,* p. 57.
56. Ibid., pp. 57-58, 59, 61.
57. Greenberg, *American Political System,* p. 471.
58. Hannah Arendt, *On Violence* (New York: Harcourt, Brace & World, 1970), p. 60.
59. Arendt, "What is Freedom?"in *Between Past and Future* (New York: Viking, 1968), p. 169.
60. Ibid., pp. 170-71.

TABLE OF CASES

ANNOTATED BIBLIOGRAPHY

Arendt, Hannah. *On Revolution.* New York: Viking Press, 1965. Arendt's analysis of revolution in the twentieth century—in particular, her examination of the American Revolution and of "public happiness"—bears on our discussion of equality.

Aristotle. *Nicomachean Ethics.* Translated by Martin Ostwald. Indianapolis: Bobbs-Merrill, 1962. In book 5 Aristotle discusses corrective justice and distributive justice and introduces the concept of "proportion" in relation to the latter.

Aristotle. *The Politics.* Translated by Ernest Barker. London: Oxford University Press, 1946. In books 4, 5, and 6 Aristotle discusses matters pertaining to equality in the context of justice, liberty, and politics. Unsurpassed in the moral philosophy of politics.

Bachrach, Peter. *The Theory of Democratic Elitism: A Critique.* Boston: Little, Brown, 1967. Bachrach criticizes contemporary theorists of democracy, such as Robert Dahl, who reject equality of political power and participation in lieu of hierarchial forms.

Bedau, Hugo, ed. *Justice and Equality.* Englewood Cliffs, N.J.: Prentice-Hall, 1971. An anthology treating justice and equality philosophically. See especially the essays by Bedau and Bernard Williams.

Bell, Daniel. "Meritocracy and Equality." *Public Interest,* Fall, 1972, pp. 29-68. Bell's neoconservative lament over the social costs of what he terms the "Tocqueville effect" in terms of decreased motivation and less concern for merit and excellence.

Best, Michael, and Connolly, William. *The Politicized Economy.* Lexington, Mass.: D.C. Heath, 1976. Good introduction to radical political economy applied to American society. Includes theoretical overview and analyses of work, the environment, inequality, and the state, among other contemporary issues.

Blumberg, Paul. *Inequality in an Age of Decline.* New York: Oxford University Press, 1980. Somber, and sobering, discussion of what happens to liberal equality when abundance is eroded by scarcity.

Boggs, Carl. *Gramsci's Marxism.* London: Pluto Press, 1976. Best available introduction to work of this seminal thinker in Marxist tradition. Gramsci influenced our analysis of equality in America especially in our treatment of proprietary equality and strategies for change.

Carnegie Council on Policy Studies in Higher Education. *Making Affirmative Action Work in Higher Education.* San Francisco: Jossey-Bass, 1975. Analysis of institutional and federal policies, with specific recommendations and discussion of potential problems.

Carnegie Council on Policy Studies in Higher Education. *Selective Admissions in Higher Eduation.* San Francisco: Jossey-Bass, 1977. Comprehensive study of selective admissions in colleges and universities. Important for understanding issues involved in *Bakke* case.

Cohen, Marshall, and Scanlon, Thomas, eds. *Equality and Preferential Treatment.* Princeton: Princeton University Press, 1977. Collection of essays dealing with variety of affirmative action issues. See especially essays by Dworkin, Goldman, Sher, Simon, and Thomson.

Edwards, Richard; Reich, Michael; and Weisskopf, Thomas, eds. *The Capitalist System.* 2d ed. Englewood Cliffs, N.J.: Prentice-Hall, 1978. Comprehensive set of essays critical of monopoly capitalism in the United States. Especially pertinent to our study are analyses of development of monopoly capitalism, its consequences for class structure and exploitation, and alternatives to the capitalist system.

Fisher, Steve, and Foster, Jim. "Models for Furthering Revolutionary Praxis in Appalachia." *Appalachian Journal* 6 (Spring, 1979): 170-194. Programmatic discussion of strategies for achieving greater equality in the Central Appalachian region of America. Expands on themes developed in chapter 9.

Green, Philip. *The Pursuit of Inequality.* New York: Pantheon Books, 1981. A critique of various contemporary apologies for inequality. Green refutes theories ranging from biological and genetic arguments to economic and philosophical defenses of hierarchy. He justifies affirmative action by appeal to the principle of political representation.

Greenberg, Edward. *Serving the Few.* New York: John Wiley, 1974. Analysis of the impact of corporate capital on government policies from a Marxist perspective. Insightful discussions of the history of the positive state, the conservative uses of liberal reform, and the maldistribution of wealth and income in America.

Harrington, Michael. *The Twilight of Capitalism.* New York: Simon & Schuster, 1976. Important discussions of Marxism, contemporary capitalism, and social policy in the United States by an influential democratic-socialist. Penetrating critique of the neoconservatives—"Adam Smith's sociology."

Hartz, Louis. *The Liberal Tradition in America.* New York: Harcourt, Brace & World, 1955. The classic analysis of the Lockean bases of American political thought, tracing the origins, development, and pervasive grip of Locke's norms.

Hobbes, Thomas. *Leviathan.* Edited by W.G. Pogson Smith. London: Oxford University Press, 1962. Standard edition of Hobbes's treatise on human nature and civil government.

Hochschild, Jennifer. *What's Fair?: American Beliefs About Distributive Justice.* Cambridge, Mass.: Harvard University Press, 1981. Despite a continuing debate over equality in the United States, there has been little significant change in the distribution of wealth over the generations. On the basis of extensive interviews, Hochschild explores facets of American ideology in the realms of private lives, the political domain, and the economic world. She finds ambivalence and no desire for economic redistribution.

Jencks, Christopher et al. *Inequality: A Reassessment of the Effect of Family and Schooling in America.* New York: Harper & Row, 1973. Controversial empirical analysis of the relationship between family background, schooling, and stratification in America. Concludes that class is more important than schooling in determining stratification.

Lewis, Michael. *The Culture of Inequality.* Amherst, Mass.: University of Massachusetts Press, 1978. Interpretive, empirical analysis of relationship between subjective views and social policy. Argues that Americans understand inequality and equality in individualized terms, holding both to be the individual's responsibility.

Locke, John. *Two Treatises of Government.* Edited by Peter Laslett. New York: Mentor Books, 1965. Standard edition of Locke's discussion of human nature, civil government, and equality.

Lukes, Steven. "Socialism and Equality." in *The Socialist Idea: A Reappraisal,* pp. 74-95, edited by Leszek Kolaowski and Stuart Hampshire. London: Quartet Books, 1977. Lays out the basic assumptions and criteria underlying a socialist conception of equality. Realistic and persuasive analysis of the egalitarian socialist position and its critics.

Macpherson, C.B. *The Political Theory of Possessive Individualism.* New York: Oxford University Press, 1964. Macpherson's provocative interpretation of English political theory as embodying the interests and world view of the rising English bourgeoisie. Controversial and suggestive.

Mansbridge, Jane. *Beyond Adversary Democracy.* New York: Basic Books, 1980. Provides a sympathetic but critical examination of the ideal of participatory ("unitary") democracy. Provocative analysis of the possibilities and limits of political equality in small democratic communities.

Marx, Karl. *Critique of the Gotha Programme.* Edited by C.P. Dutt. New York: International Publishers, 1966. Marx's commentary on the 1875 Programme of the German Workers' Party. Marx deals here with equality most explicitly, criticizing the liberal understanding of equality and explaining socialist and communist equality by contrast.

Miliband, Ralph. *Marxism and Politics.* New York: Oxford University Press, 1977. Concise, cogent introduction to Marxist political theory. Deals with such central topics as Marxist definition of the working class, the state, the "dictatorship of the proletariat," as well as the difference between reform and revolution.

Pennock, J.R., and Chapman, J.W., eds. *Equality: Nomos IX.* New York: Atherton, 1967. Influential, important collection of essays dealing with equality in philosophical and political terms. See especially essays by Bedau, Benn, Plamenatz, and Schaar.

Rae, Douglas, et al. *Equalities.* Cambridge, Mass.: Harvard University Press, 1981. With the aid of an ingenious "grammar of equality" the authors discuss different types of equalities which are functions of context. In their view, the question is not *whether* to pursue equality but *which* equality to pursue.

Rainwater, Lee, ed. *Inequality and Justice.* Chicago: Aldine, 1974. Anthology treating various public policy aspects of relationship between inequality and justice. Comprehensive analysis of social policy aspects of equality in America. See especially essays by Rainwater and essay by Dahrendorf.

Rawls, John. *A Theory of Justice.* Cambridge: Harvard University Press, 1971. Much-debated, very influential treatise on assumptions and prerequisites of justice in a liberal society. Rawl's analysis of equality has influenced our own.

Ryan, William. *Equality.* New York: Pantheon Books, 1981. In an analysis complementary to our own, Ryan analyzes the predicament of many millions of Americans who either presently live in economic jeopardy or are threatened by it. An eloquent statement on behalf of what Michael Harrington called the other America. Questions, as we do, the ideological bases of inequality.

Tocqueville, Alex de. *Democracy in America.* 2 vols. Edited by Henry Reeve, Translated by Phillips Bradley. New York: Vintage Books, 1945. Standard edition of Tocqueville's penetrating analysis of "democracy" (by which he meant equality) in America. Traces circumstances supporting as well as those eroding equality in early nineteenth-century American life. Remains timely.

United States Commission on Civil Rights. *Statement on Affirmative Action.* Washington, D.C., 1977. Original source for regulations governing affirmative action pursuant to Title VI of the Civil Rights Act of 1964.

United States Equal Employment Opportunity Commission. *Affirmative Action and Equal Employment: A Guidebook for Employers.* Washington, D.C., 1974. Original source for requirements and regulations governing equal employment opportunity pursuant to Executive Order 11246 (1965) issued by President Lyndon B. Johnson.

Walzer, Michael. "In Defense of Equality." in *The New Conservatives,* pp. 107-123, edited by Lewis Coser and Irving Howe. New York: New American Library, 1973. Brilliant, persuasive essay defending the nature and importance of equality among human beings. Argues that genuine equality requires a diversity of criteria and proportional treatment.

Wilson, John. *Equality*. New York: Harcourt, Brace & World, 1966. Sophisticated analytical inquiry into assumptions underlying arguments about equality. Helpful in sorting out different conceptions of equality.

INDEX

Affirmative action, 5-6; history of, 45-54; term first used, 49; Philadelphia Plan and use of quotas, 50; defined, 50; rational for, 50-51; operation of, 51; controversy over, 52-53; and equal educational opportunity, 55-62; 63; and equal employment opportunity, 63-73; and Title VII, Civil Rights Act of 1964, 65; various justifications of, 75-87; three categories of justification summarized, 75-76; definition recapitulated, 76; and equal opportunity doctrine, 77-78; and utilitarian justifications, 78-80; and compensatory justice justifications, 80-96; five elements of adequate justification of, 86-87; evaluating effectiveness of, 89-97; applied to federal government, 91-92; recurring problems with, 92-95; limitations of, 95-96; assessment of summarized, 96-97.

Alevy v. *Downstate Medical Center* (1976), 66.

Arendt, Hannah, 24, 25; on human freedom to choose, 134-135.

Aristotle, on corrective justice, 81-82; on distributive (proportional) justice, 131.

Babbitt, 5.

Bedeau, Hugo A., 107, 108, 110.

Bell, Daniel, 46, 126; on "Tocqueville effect," 127.

Best, Michael, 118, 120; 127-128; 132-133.

Bittker, Boris, 82-83.

Blumberg, Paul, 116.

Brown v. *Board of Education of Topeka* (1954), 61, 112.

Brown, Justice Henry, 112.

Burnham, Walter Dean, 124.

Capital, Das, 121.

Carnegie, Andrew, 33; 37-39.

Case for Black Reparations, The, 82.

Cleaver, Harry, 121; 133-134.

Commonwealth of Pennsylvania v. *Rizzo* (1975), 52.

Compensatory justice, as justification for affirmative action, 80-86.

Connolly, William, 101, 118, 120; 127-128; 132-133.

Corfield v. *Coryell* (1923), 36.

Cramer v. *Virginia Commonwealth University* (1976), 67.

Crevecoeur, Hector St. John de, 24.

Critique of the Gotha Program, 120-121.

Culture of inequality, 5; defined, 40; analyzed in relation to proprietary equality, 40-41; 134.

Dahl, Robert, 105, 125.

Dartmouth College v. *Woodward* (1819), 32.

Davis, Kingsley, 127-128.

Deane, Herbert, 83.

Declaration of Independence, 24, 116; and ontological equality, 118-119.

De Funis v. *Odegaard* (1974), 66, 113.

Democratic socialism, and equality, 132; as a strategy for obtaining equality, 132-134.

Diamond, Martin, 13.

Discourse on the Origin of Inequality, 104.

Drew, Daniel, 37-38.

Dworkin, Ronald, 113.

Edelman, Murray, 18.

Equal Employment Opportunity Act of 1972, 65.